WORTH

EVERY

SECOND

WORTH

EVERY

SECOND

Developing Perseverance in Our Faith

JENNIFER CADAMORE

For Yeshua.

Speaking Your name does something
indescribable to my soul.

Living for You is pure joy.

Table of Contents

ACKNOWLEDGEMENTS

I praise God for Who He is. Without His wisdom and provision, this book never would have been possible. Every single word is His inspiration and to Him be the glory.

I also thank Him for blessing me with the most amazing family. I am so grateful for their support and I don't take for granted how well loved I am.

Brian, thank you for your patience when I'd come to bed late after writing and wake you up. I tried so hard not to do that but inevitably, I'd drop something or run into a door which, remarkably, is in exactly the same place it's always been. Thank you for persevering through life with me. I'd have it no other way.

Ben, thank you for your insights, advice and encouragement throughout this project. Your gifts and willingness to help have blessed me more than you know. Quinn, I'm so happy you've come into our family. You bring such joy.

Matthew and Meghan, thank you for having impeccable timing in knowing when to call, visit or send a hilarious video, especially those starring our precious new granddaughter,

Frankie. You have no idea how much a diversion of family and laughter was needed throughout the writing process.

John, thank you for allowing me to share your own personal story of perseverance. Andrea, thank you for walking so beautifully beside my son during this ongoing challenge.

Finally, because there is some content regarding canines within the pages of this book and he's also a beloved member of our family, I'd be remiss if I didn't mention Gus, our wonderful pooch, whose faithful and calming presence next to me during the many hours of writing has made me decide to confess something. John, Matt and Ben: in your speculation of who might be my favorite, I've always told you guys that I don't have one. Actually, I do—it's Gus. Now you know.

My dear, sweet family, I pray that you will continue to persevere. I love each of you deeply and for eternity. xoxo

Make a joyful noise to the Lord, all the earth!
2 Serve the Lord with gladness!
Come into his presence with singing!

3 Know that the Lord, he is God!
It is he who made us, and we are his;
we are his people, and the sheep of his pasture.

4 Enter his gates with thanksgiving,
and his courts with praise!
Give thanks to him; bless his name!

5 For the Lord is good; his steadfast love endures forever,
and his faithfulness to all generations.

Psalm 100

trib·u·la·tion

/ˌtribyəˈlāSH(ə)n/

Noun

plural noun: tribulations

: distress or suffering resulting from oppression or persecution also: a trying experience [1]

per·se·ver·ance

/ˌpərsəˈvirəns/

Noun

: continued effort to do or achieve something despite difficulties, failure, or opposition: the action or condition or
an instance of persevering: steadfastness [2]

WORTH EVERY SECOND

:01

Electricity

When I reflect on my younger years, I see a striking similarity between electricity and the paths in life I preferred to take. I'm not really qualified enough to delve into all the science-y stuff of electricity so I won't. Let's just agree on the most basic level that electricity takes the path of least resistance.

Also me, in any and every difficult circumstance.

Waiting was never my specialty. Technically, it still isn't but the trait is maturing as I learn a thing or two along the way. Like every other person on the planet, the reality is that life is more akin to static electricity, and here's a short lesson on that: it's the result of an imbalance between negative and positive charges in an object wherein the electrons will move about in sudden, uncontrollable ways. The correlation? Life is a series of events that often happen suddenly over which we have no control. Some events we want, others not so much. Regardless of this being an obvious truth, I inevitably rejected the not so much ones for the path that wouldn't shake things up. No confrontations. No hard work. No digging deeper to learn something new. Just give it to me quick and easy and don't make me wait for it. No matter the cost, no matter if I'm selling my soul.

Talk about an imbalance.

And let me remind you, this was all *before* current-day instant gratification with asking Google to answer our questions, Alexa to play our favorite song or social media notifications that tell us who liked or responded to our post. As it is with so many of this generation, decades ago I was addicted to the rush of getting everything quickly without waiting one extra second more than I had to. I guess you could say I was a bit of a trailblazer.

If I wanted something but couldn't afford it, I charged it to a credit card. If only the money I spent on all of those shoes and clothes I just "had" to have was used for college or given to charity.

If I wanted to do well on a test, I'd study but then rather than face the fact that I couldn't remember it all and learn something through failure, I'd cheat in order to get the grade I wanted. Of course, the gratification of earning something I didn't really earn wasn't gratifying at all.

If I wanted a guy to like me, I'd become whatever it was he wanted me to be. It never grew any healthy relationships but, instead, always left me burned and lonely.

If things seemed to be going too slowly for my liking in whatever situation, I'd manipulate the circumstances or push until I got what I wanted because, after all, I "deserved" it. Because gee whiz, otherwise it would take patience. Who has time for that?!

I shake my head in disbelief when I think of some of the ridiculous attitudes I had and the monumental mistakes I made because of them. "Like a gold ring in a pig's snout, is a beautiful woman who lacks discretion" (Proverbs 11:22, NIV). I can tell you, I did not encompass nor embrace discretion because that would require me to *take time* to be wise. "If any of you lacks wisdom, let him ask God, who gives generously to all without reproach, and it will be given him" (James 1:5).

I had no convictions of my own because it was simply easier to follow what others did; thus, I was "tossed to and fro by the waves and carried about by every wind of doctrine, by human cunning, by craftiness in deceitful schemes" (Ephesians 4:14).

Being challenged and held accountable was met with outright resistance because it made me feel inferior. Having to face my shortcomings and enact change was too uncomfortable. So, I didn't. The result of having this kind of mindset carried consequences then and it always will.

Because I didn't seek out wisdom, my life was filled with chaos, anxiety, defensiveness, insecurity and childish fits of anger, generously peppered with profanity.

Because I followed others, I had no leadership skills.

Because I didn't want to put forth the effort to even consider putting aside unhealthy behaviors, I missed being all God created me to be.

I was a ship at sea with no oars, no sails and no compass.

Floating around aimlessly got me nowhere fast and caused more shipwrecks than I can count. (Why a nautical theme here? Why not a nautical theme?)

In retrospect, I know why I was this way: I didn't have Jesus as my guide.

What a travesty that I felt nothing was ever worth the

cost or that nothing of value came in doing things God's way, according to His plan, on His timeline.

But that was then, this is now. Today I'm what I like to call a "reformed entitle-ist" and I no longer believe that I deserve to have everything I want when I want it and how I want it. The lies and fears of my youth (and teens and early twenties) have been thrown overboard.

Praise be to God for 2 Corinthians 5:17 that affirms, "Therefore, if anyone is in Christ, he is a new creation. The old has passed away; behold, the new has come." I am a new creation! I am now in Christ and He is in me. He gave His life for me and the day I surrendered mine to Him will forever be the best day of my life. Many days have come close but never will any top it. That is, until, I see my Savior face to face. In his book, *Unshakeable Hope*, Max Lucado tells believers that "Your finest moment will be your final moment."[3] That's the hope we have in Jesus, that this life, with all its beautiful and blessed moments intertwined with pain and sorrow gets *way* better. Just hang on. You'll see. We are citizens of Heaven, living here for the time being. I'm looking forward to moving day.

Is my life easier because I chose Jesus? No. Are you

surprised by that answer? Let me tell you why you shouldn't be: The second part of John 16:33 tells us, "In the world you will have tribulation. But take heart; I have overcome the world." Because I chose Jesus, the first part of the Scripture is far better than an easy life: "I have said these things to you, that in me you may have peace." I want peace in my heart more than ease in my life so I make a decision each day to *take time* to seek wisdom. I choose the less popular and often more ridiculed path of following Jesus instead of the world. I am now comfortable with the static in my life because I know that God is steadily working to grow my faith, especially in the midst of the difficulties. I am able to confidently say that I know He will carry me safely through the storms. Isaiah 43:1-2 offers this promise: "But now thus says the LORD, he who created you, O Jacob, he who formed you, O Israel: 'Fear not, for I have redeemed you; I have called you by name, you are mine. When you pass through the waters, I will be with you; and through the rivers, they shall not overwhelm you; when you walk through fire you shall not be burned, and the flame shall not consume you.'"

Who doesn't want to live without fear? Or have the confidence that no situation will consume or overwhelm them? Who doesn't want to know that they belong? That

6

they will be protected? Who doesn't want to know how to accomplish these things, right? Well, this isn't a self-help book. I'm not the person who is qualified to lay out all the steps you need to take in each of your personal experiences. There's no way I can do that. I'm not sovereign or omnipotent or omnipresent.

This book is about pointing you toward the only One who can offer true peace and guide you down the path He created for you. It's about highlighting the Bible, the unchanging Word of God, which has been given to us to help navigate this life here on earth and prepare us for Heaven. If it's anything, it is a "God-help" book so that you look to Him for assistance, with every breath and every fiber of your being, all the days of your life. He longs for us to seek His standard about everything we face and, oh, what phenomenal results when we do! He desires that we receive what He has given us so that we may give to others. That's how we share Jesus, how we live out Matthew 28:19-20, "Go therefore and make disciples of all nations, baptizing them in the name of the Father and of the Son and of the Holy Spirit, teaching them to observe all that I have commanded you. And behold, I am with you always, to the end of the age."

When I consider my earlier years, I think that the reason I didn't seek wisdom or discretion or redemption was because I didn't know I lacked it. I'd venture to say that I didn't even care if I did. I suppose on one level I believed I possessed it. That's dangerous stuff right there. "Be not wise in your own eyes; fear the Lord, and turn away from evil" (Proverbs 3:7).

The first time I had been asked to attend a Women of Faith conference in Pittsburgh, I was exceptionally nervous. Generally speaking, my perception of anyone who talked about Jesus or quoted Scripture was a Bible toting, holy-roller Jesus freak whose sole purpose was to make others feel bad about their sins. I had lived a pretty sheltered life, spiritually speaking, and had never been a part of youth group, mission work or a Bible study to this point in my life. I had no idea what to expect when a bunch of Christian women got together. But God did and He knew what would happen later that evening.

I rode down with my cousin and three other women, all of whom had been walking with Jesus for a much longer time than I had been. Since insecurity was always at the forefront of my experiences, especially in new scenarios like this, I was feeling really out of place. But as the conversations flowed about their life stories, I was put at ease and realized that any negative, preconceived notions I had about Christianity were unfounded. We were all just a bunch of women trying to navigate life, sometimes getting it right and sometimes not.

One woman shared an incredibly tragic story that turned out to be her salvation story. She was young, unmarried and pregnant. She and the father made the decision to terminate the pregnancy. As she lay on the table, her unborn baby's life ending, she prayed the Lord's prayer. She sobbed and sobbed and asked God to forgive her and surrendered to Him right there in the abortion clinic. I had never in my life heard anyone be so open about their sin and I had never, ever thought God was *that* forgiving. After all, weren't there levels of sin? Wasn't this the worst of the worst? But no, the atmosphere in that car was unlike anything I had ever experienced. There was redemption and yes, joy. Not over the killing of an unborn soul but because of Jesus.

With unfathomable love and mercy, He received both that little baby and its mother unto Himself at the same time. Whew.

That story led me to ask about sin and God's grace. Don't we need to earn our way to Heaven? I mean, I know a lot of nice people. Won't they make it based on their being nice? I remember my cousin explaining to me that is not how it works, that it is only through our acceptance of Christ's sacrifice that we go to Heaven. We can't earn it and we don't deserve it. But, "God shows his love for us in that while we were still sinners, Christ died for us. [9] Since, therefore, we have now been justified by his blood, much more shall we be saved by him from the wrath of God" (Romans 5:8-9). We are only made worthy by the One Who is worthy. She went on to add, "There's going to be a lot of 'nice' people in Hell." I've never forgotten that.

The conference was incredible. I thought it was a good sign that when I walked in to the venue there was a banner with the first Scripture verse I had ever memorized. At that time it was the only one.

"Let everything that has breath praise the LORD" (Psalm 150:6).

After that, I could never have anticipated the contrast of the event to what I was used to. At the time, I was part of a denomination in which the services were rigid and ritualistic; we did not raise our hands into the air, nor did we sway, shout out "Amen" or sing upbeat songs. We went, we did, we left. I mean no disrespect to that denomination, not at all. I'm just sharing my experience with the two very different worship styles.

I didn't know a lot of the songs they sang at the event but it didn't matter. I was moved. Something stirred inside my heart that night and I felt freer and more alive than I ever had in any church environment. I know now that the Holy Spirit was present in that building and He was preparing me for what God would speak to me when I got home.

Our ride back was filled with excited chatter as we shared what each speaker had said that encouraged or convicted us. There were more stories, more questions and lots of laughter. I didn't want the night to end. By the time I got home, I was so pumped up that I felt like I was about to burst.

But, alas, as is always the case when we're drawing closer to God, Satan wants to thwart any and all forward progress. No doubt he had been scheming all night and was eager to destroy my newfound joy. Now that I was alone, away from the support of the women I had spent the evening worshipping God with, it was time for him to make his move. I envision him salivating at the mouth, rubbing his hands together while inside of him a sick, twisted rush of adrenaline occurs as he initiates his plan of attack.

I hate him so much.

I took my shoes off, hung up my coat and since it was

late and my family was asleep, I sat down at the dining room table to ponder all that had happened.

Suddenly, I began to feel overwhelmed. This is where the whisper of doubt—that *only* comes from the evil one—made me weep over how little I knew about God and His Word. I felt confused and inadequate. I was quickly losing the excitement I had carried with me less than ten minutes before.

I did the only thing I knew to do in that moment and that was to pray. *God, this is all so new to me. I don't know what to do or how to do it. Please show me.* I looked across the table, saw my Bible and pulled it before me. I sat for a moment just staring at it. *Lord, what do you want me to read right now?* I still ask Him that when I don't know where to begin.

And here's what He had been waiting to show me all night, all my life, really, from Proverbs 2:3-10:

"Yes, if you want better insight and discernment, and are searching for them as you would for lost money or hidden treasure, then wisdom will be given you and knowledge of God himself; you will soon learn the importance of reverence for the Lord and of trusting him. [6] For the Lord grants wisdom! His every word is a treasure of knowledge and understanding. [7-8] He grants good sense to the godly—his saints. He is their shield, protecting them and guarding their pathway. [9] He shows how to distinguish right from wrong, how to find the right decision every time. [10] For wisdom and truth will enter the very center of your being, filling your life with joy" (TLB).

I was already born again, but as the words came alive to me, this moment in time would be the pivotal point in my study of the Bible. I'd still have many more of these moments and I know as long as I'm on this side of eternity I'll have many more significant revelations that lead to the next step in my faith. But oh, this was the missing piece of the puzzle. It clicked perfectly and launched me into doing the hard work. I just needed to ask. Gee, what a novel idea. God has lots of them, by the way.

Truly, it was breathtaking. I couldn't wrap my mind around how clearly He had just spoken to me. If I hadn't believed that God actually spoke to us through the Bible before that, I certainly did now. I had asked and He had answered. Admittedly, in true Jennifer fashion, I was appreciative I didn't have to wait long. To say I was speechless is an understatement and if you know me well, it's also unbelievable. He knew what would transpire in those few short hours on that chilly fall night.

What's hard to fathom is that He had been waiting for me to arrive there. Just like He had waited for me to invite Him into my life. Just like how He still waits to talk with me. He's always wanting us to seek, always waiting for us to step out and always already there to meet us when we do. This relationship is like no other we will ever encounter. The unconditional love, unending grace and boundless mercy He has for us far exceeds anything we can comprehend.

If electricity flows better without things in its way or struggles when there are, it's easy to understand why people say it will seek the path that resists less. But while I understand it, I don't recommend it. My hope and prayer is that you'll do the exact opposite of what I did all those years ago and won't always try to find the path of least resistance. Please don't be electricity. Do the hard stuff. Embrace stretching, God's timing and difficult, uncomfortable situations. There is no guarantee of an easy life but there is a guarantee of an everlasting one spent in the presence of Jesus if you choose to have a relationship with Him.

I pray you'll *take time* to ask what the Lord would want you to do in the big and small things of your life. Think of the most valuable possession you have and the lengths you'd go to finding it if you lost it. Seek out wisdom, discretion and direction in the same way. I promise, it's worth every second.

:02

Mini Van

If GPS devices had actually existed way back then, my saved list of favorites would have only consisted of one address: 123 Easy Street, Anytown, USA. The funny/not funny thing is, if I had just faced the difficult, uncomfortable situations head-on, I wouldn't have wasted so much of my energy going in circles.

If you've ever read the comic strip *The Family Circus*, written by Bil Keane, little Billy often tells his mom he's just going to go from point A to point B but the actual path he travels is illustrated as a jumbled mess of lines, suggesting he went to point Z instead. That was the chaos I created in my life and the waste of time was anything but comical. I missed a cache of beneficial life lessons in failing to seek God's path for me. And believe me when I say that it happened repeat-edly.

WORTH EVERY SECOND

I'd like to preface the following story with this: I am not and never have been driven by money or materialism. That's not to say I don't like money or things; I do enjoy some luxuries but I'm a pretty simple girl with simple tastes. My greatest pleasures come from things money cannot buy, like family, sunsets, flowers, birds and laughter. Good, hearty laughter. But the following story is an example of what can happen when we lose our focus. The solution is to not lose sight of what's most important: Jesus.

When we were building our home, I had a Ford Taurus that was on its last leg. It had seen many miles and better days. It wasn't as trustworthy as it used to be but being a stay-at-home mom with another vehicle in our family, it wasn't necessarily at the top of the list of things to buy. After all, we needed to buy paint and cupboards and countertops and appliances for our new home. And perhaps a jacuzzi tub. Building a home isn't cheap and neither are vehicles.

At one point, it seemed as if we were going to be forced to have to go car shopping because many nights Brian would come home at 11 p.m. and have to fix the car, after building a house for a customer during regular business hours and building ours in the evening. I praise God he is gifted with

18

the ability to fix just about anything and I prayed that it would last us a little while longer so we wouldn't have to deal with car shopping while construction was taking place. We didn't need any distractions. One massive undertaking at a time, thank you.

To be honest, though, I was starting to get excited about the possibilities. Over the course of days and months, daydreaming about it became a favorite pastime of mine. Since we didn't have a computer at the time, I studied cars on the roadway and stopped at dealerships, when they weren't open. No sense in getting their hopes up since we simply weren't ready to take the next step. Ultimately, I became increasingly convinced we should get a minivan because it would be the most logical and affordable for a family of four, with room to grow if necessary. I was adamant that I wanted a black one with a gray interior with no need for too much automatic stuff. When it comes to automobiles, I don't need it to be bedazzled or fancy; I just need it to start and then transport me to my destination. But the color was important because I knew I'd be driving it for years to come and it had to be something that I wouldn't tire of.

When I presented the idea to Brian, he was fine with all

of it. And that, my friends, was a mistake. Now that we were both on board, I brought it up in conversation any chance I got, even interjecting the idea into conversations that had nothing to do with any mode of travel—express, implied or otherwise. "Mom, what's the name of that black bird in the yard?" one of the kids might ask at dinner. "That's a crow, honey. Brian, that reminds me, did you know the Dodge Grand Caravan has *Stow-n-Go* seats? Can you believe they fold down into the floor?!" (Seriously, that's genius.)

By the time we were ready to move in to our home, I was agitated about not having my dream car. I grew increasingly impatient (if you've been paying attention, this shouldn't surprise you) and it seemed to me that over the next four years God was actively trying to torture me. Brian's work vehicle died a quick death and we had to search for a truck for him. Really? I have to wait even longer now? I'm not proud of my foolish behavior, by the way.

After we purchased the company truck, my trusty Taurus still limping along, I found I was getting bitter. Sadly, I adopted a life-isn't-fair-and-everyone-has-it-better-than-me-and-I'm-never-going-to-get-my-new-minivan-*ever* attitude. While I had surrendered my life to Jesus as Lord, I was still learning how to take my thoughts captive. As a novice, it was two steps forward and four, maybe five, steps back. But I was working at it and determined to choose what God would want. I had the Holy Spirit working on the inside, helping me to take the next step in my faith day after day, month after month. I can only imagine what God protected me from because besides the fact that I'm human and we humans are sinners, the bottom line is as a follower of Jesus, I was, by default, a target for Satan. In retrospect, I'm grateful he annoyed me so much because each time he lied to me, I had to go back to God for strength and guidance. It drew me closer to the Father! Isn't that awesome?

I remember feeling grateful I even had a car to drive but as is often the case when we're fixated on one thing, instead of on The One, my frustration outweighed my gratitude.

What a terrible road to go down. (No pun intended.)

Not long after, we were blessed with our third son. Knowing that my vehicle wouldn't allow for three car seats with shoulder straps in the back seat, I knew that we'd have to get a different vehicle by the time he would be front-facing. But being busy with a newborn plus two other active boys, there wasn't a whole lot of time to be crying the blues over a car. It's just a car, after all.

When my neighbors innocently drove down the road in their new minivan one day, jealousy rose up in me. *That's not fair! I've been waiting for how long for one!* Shortly thereafter, my brother and sister-in-law pushed me over the edge when they bought one of their own. *What the heck? They don't even need one!* I was baffled. *God, why?*

The answer, I came to find out, was to expand my spiritual horizons and my ability to cope with life's unfair and frustrating events. This silly obsession that had caused me to at times to think and act like a fool, was, in fact, for my benefit. With God, it always is.

"In this you rejoice, though now for a little while, if necessary, you have been grieved by various trials, so that the tested genuineness of your faith—more precious than gold that perishes though it is tested by fire—may be found to result in praise and glory and honor at the revelation of Jesus Christ" (1 Peter 1:6-7).

My neighbors continued to flaunt their shiny new minivan past our house each day. I understood they had to go to work but I thought it was a bit much to take the same route not just once, upon leaving, but twice; apparently, they also had to come home. Couldn't they find another country road? Why did they hate me so much? I thought we were friends.

What's so interesting is that while He was teaching me about patience, I was also being taught about the sin of envy. Maybe you caught on to that but I missed it.

"You shall not covet your neighbor's house; you shall not covet your neighbor's wife, or his male servant, or his female servant, or his ox, or his donkey, or anything that is your neighbor's" (Exodus 20:17; Deuteronomy 5:21). All of our neighbors have houses and I was okay with that. Incidentally, because we live in the country, some of our neighbors actually do own livestock. If they had gotten more, I wouldn't have cared one bit. Get all the four-legged animals and two-legged fowl you want. But for the love of Pete, not a minivan.

The tenth commandment should've immediately come to mind but I was busy dealing with patience. One principle at a time, please. That's the interesting thing about the pruning process: while one thing is being lopped off, another is about to meet the same fate. He'll use lessons about one issue across multiple feelings, emotions and situations in order to strengthen commitments and convictions. I learned so many things within this one circumstance I am able to draw on the insights again and again and again, in perpetuity. That's Who God is and that's what He does.

During this time, I took feelings, behaviors and character traits that I knew needed tweaking (some needed outright eliminating) and used the Word of God to combat each one, developing into a mini booklet of verse after verse, organized by subject. I still use it as a resource.

One of the verses that I had to recite over and over was Romans 13:12-14, "The night is far gone, the day of his return will soon be here. So quit the evil deeds of darkness and put on the armor of right living, as we who live in the daylight should! Be decent and true in everything you do so that all can approve your behavior. Don't spend your time in wild parties and getting drunk or in adultery and lust or fighting or jealousy. But ask the Lord Jesus Christ to help you live as you should, and don't make plans to enjoy evil" (TLB).

What had spoken to me so clearly was that I wasn't supposed to spend my time being jealous but was to ask the Lord how to live as I should.

Because I continued to use the Word of God instead of my feelings, I began to see a shift in my behavior and an inner peace. Now when I saw my neighbors in their new minivan, I prayed for them. I asked God to keep them safe in it. I asked that they would have the funds to pay for it and any expenses it incurred. I thanked Him that they were able to get what their family needed. Can you believe that? But that's what God can do—and did do.

Having waited almost six years, I'm not kidding when I say that within two months my black Dodge Grand Caravan (with *Stow-n-Go* seats!) sat in my garage. I know that the reason I had to wait was for God to get me to a point of surrender in order to work past the jealousy and idolatry. Yes, when we spend our time thinking about something or someone more than we think on God, we have given those things more importance and that's idolatry. Exodus 20:3 tells us, "You shall have no other gods before me." A hunk of metal on four wheels had become a god to me.

I share this story as a stark reminder of what 1 Peter 5:8 tells us: "Be sober-minded; be watchful. Your adversary the devil prowls around like a roaring lion, seeking someone to devour."

Whatever your reality is right now, I warn you of this: don't give the devil a foothold (Ephesians 4:27) by giving your flesh permission to continue in sin. Do not put people, places, things (or lack of any of them) first on your heart's pedestal, thereby making them your gods. Only the One True God deserves the top spot. Ask God on a daily basis to reveal what sins are lurking inside of you. Don't be afraid to hear the Truth; it's so rich in blessings to be able to know what we need to repent of! Since sin separates us from God, why *wouldn't* we want to know? (Note: This doesn't mean we lose our salvation because of sin; Christ died on the cross for each one and we are eternally sealed when we accept His sacrifice.) Even as a born-again believer, we're still capable of straying from doing what's right. When we do, we need to acknowledge our sin and seek forgiveness. The good news is, "If we confess our sins, he is faithful and just to forgive us our sins and to cleanse us from all unrighteousness" (1 John 1:9). I want to be cleansed. I need to be cleansed.

Paul instructs his listeners then and readers today, "Finally, be strong in the Lord and in the strength of his might. Put on the whole armor of God, that you may be able to stand against the schemes of the devil" (Ephesians 6:10-11).

When jealousy rears its ugly head, this is one of the

verses I immediately speak out to the evil one. I refuse to give in to something that I know is not right living and I know the power God's Word has over the devil's mutterings.

As Christians, it's so important to know the Truth found in the Bible. It's imperative to hold it tightly in our hearts and to use it as our defense. It's necessary for keeping our motives and thoughts in check because in our humanness, we can go down paths that aren't the best God has for us.

I'm so grateful for His grace and mercy that carry me through my not-so-shining moments.

Dear, sweet soul, please don't underestimate the power the Scriptures can (and will) have in your life. Please heed my words of caution: don't skimp on studying the inerrant Word of God. The time and effort are worth every second.

:03

Jesus Is No Quitter

May I get personal with you? What's eating at you today? What are you struggling with? What kept you up last night? What have you fervently been praying about for the last month or past ten years?

I want you to think of that thing, that person, that burden that's been on your mind, causing the same emotions to keep resurfacing and the knot in your stomach to remain.

With that difficulty in mind, I want to take a look at Romans 4:18 – 5:4 but first provide a quick background to the story. Paul is planning to visit the Christian church in Rome, something no apostle had done before. He writes this letter to the believers there in preparation for his visit, sharing the Gospel message.

In this portion of scripture, he is using Abraham's struggle with not having a son (from Genesis 15) to illustrate how disappointment or a difficult circumstance doesn't have to weaken our faith but can be used to strengthen it. God promised Abraham that he was going to give him a son, and although it seemed absurd that it could happen at his advanced age, Abraham chose to believe in God's ability. It seemed he had a little more trouble trusting in His timing, though.

If you know the story, in his impatience (and humanness), he takes matters into his own hands, maybe believing it was what God wanted him to do or maybe because his wife Sarah was very convincing. Either way and is always the case, his actions had consequences. But God, as is always the case, was still faithful and kept His promise (Abraham and Sarah had Isaac).

Turning our attention back to Paul's letter, he reiterates, "In hope he believed against hope, that he should become the father of many nations, as he had been told, "So shall your offspring be." [19] He did not weaken in faith when he considered his own body, which was as good as dead (since he was about a hundred years old), or when he considered the barrenness of Sarah's womb. [20] No unbelief made him waver concerning the promise of God, but he grew strong in his faith as he gave glory to God, [21] fully convinced that God was able to do what he had promised. [22] That is why his faith was "counted to him as righteousness." [23] But the words "it was counted to him" were not written for his sake alone, [24] but for ours also. It will be counted to us who believe in him who raised from the dead Jesus our Lord, [25] who was delivered up for our trespasses and raised for our justification...[1] Therefore, since we have been justified by faith, we have peace with God through our Lord Jesus Christ. [2] Through him we have also obtained access by faith into this grace in which we stand, and we rejoice in hope of the glory of God. [3] Not only that, but we rejoice in our sufferings, knowing that suffering produces endurance, [4] and endurance produces character, and character produces hope..."

The verse begins with the reference to Abraham: who, against all hope, and despite the fact that he and Sarah were very old, believed he would have a child and many descendants. He did not waver in his belief, verse 20 says, but was strengthened and able to persevere because he was "*fully persuaded that God had power to do what he had promised.*" (Italics mine.)

Do you struggle with being fully persuaded that God has the power to work through your difficult circumstance?

31

Maybe you believe God has the power but you may struggle with the patience part, waiting for God to work things through and out. I hope by the end of this book—by the end of this chapter—you'll have a better perspective and a renewed hope in regard to that burden. So, whatever you're waiting for, I encourage you to not give up, do not take matters into your own hands nor entertain the idea of manipulating the situation (or people) to make the outcome happen sooner. There are always consequences to trying to get ahead of God. He will keep His promise to see you through. "He who calls you is faithful; he will surely do it" (1 Thessalonians 5:24).

He. Is. Faithful.

Allow me to remind you of Easter, a joyful day in which believers celebrate that after Jesus Christ was crucified—willingly—He was then "raised to life for our justification" (v. 25). Hallelujah! BUT FIRST—He was "delivered over to death for our sins" (v. 25). *Our* sins. Jesus was sinless. "For we do not have a high priest who is unable to sympathize with our weaknesses, but one who in every respect has been tempted as we are, yet without sin" (Hebrews 4:15).

We are grateful and I would venture to say, relieved, to be honest, that we, through faith, don't have to endure what

He did.

Jesus' road to the cross was anything but easy. He was misunderstood, betrayed, mocked, persecuted, rejected, spat on, whipped, beaten, and was nailed to a cross to die an excruciating death. For you. For me. For every human being ever born or yet to be.

With that in mind, imagine this horrible scenario: what if Jesus had quit? What if He had decided the journey was just too hard? Who could blame Him, really?

Let's look at Romans 5, verses 1 and 2 again: we love that we're justified, that we have peace with God by faith, in other words, because of what Jesus did. We love that He grants us grace, which is the beautiful, unmerited favor of God, and we have hope because God is faithful in keeping His promises.

Hope is defined as, "to desire with expectation of obtainment or fulfillment; to expect with confidence: trust." [2] Hope is what Abraham had because he was persuaded that God would do what He said He would. We could even say that he had hope against hope, which is, "to hope without any basis for expecting fulfillment." [3]

Justified. Peace. Grace. Hope.

These are some feel-good words, aren't they? This is all

the wonderful part of our faith, right? We can get on board with all of these and raise a "hallelujah!" because these are easy.

But then there's verse three, "Not only so, but we also glory in our sufferings..." Wait, what? Glory in our sufferings? Um, I don't think so and no thank you anyway. *Glory* is defined as "adoring praise or worshipful thanksgiving; to exult with triumph and great beauty and splendor: magnificence; something marked by beauty or resplendence; the splendor and beatific happiness of heaven, broadly: eternity." [5]

We're told in 1 Peter 4:12-13, "Beloved, do not be surprised at the fiery trial when it comes upon you to test you, as though something strange were happening to you. [13] But rejoice insofar as you share Christ's sufferings, that you may also rejoice and be glad when his glory is revealed."

Are you glory-ing in your sufferings? How about in the burden I had you think about?

How in the world can we equate our sufferings with adoring praise, worshipful thanksgiving, view them as splendid, majestic or beautiful amidst—and despite—them?

The answer is found in the last part of the verse: "because we know that our suffering produces perseverance; perseverance, character; and character, hope." We look at each

34

difficulty using the broad definition of glory, in light of eternity. We can't do this on our own so God gave us the help of the Holy Spirit and He'll give us His perspective, too.

See, God is in the business of developing in us very important components to our faith. It is a process that helps us to continue stepping forward and developing those all-important Christ-like character traits. That process is called *sanctification* and it means "to make holy; set apart as sacred; consecrate." [6] Remember, when we accept Christ as our Savior, we enter into an agreement with him. We say, *Lord, I give You my life to use as You see fit because You gave Your life for me*. When that happens, we begin "growing in divine grace as a result of Christian commitment after baptism or conversion" [7] and it's something that doesn't stop—shouldn't stop—while we're on this side of Heaven.

God's ultimate purpose is to make us more like Christ so that we can carry out HIS will for our lives so that we can have an impact on other people's lives. It's not something we can do in our own power therefore, God is going to have to purify us through the power of the Holy Spirit and we have to learn to accept that he will do it on HIS terms.

Oftentimes, the way He does it isn't in the pretty little box we'd like it to be in. Life is hard. We experience grief, hurt, frustration and disappointment. If we had our way, we'd rather a straight line between two points of joy without any detours in the middle. Like me. Like electricity.

But let me sweetly remind each of you (and I have to remind myself sometimes, as well) that God is not interested too much in making sure your life is easy and from a human perspective what we would consider perfect. Scripture says it won't be.

"I have told you these things, so that in me you may have peace. In this world you will have trouble. But take heart! I have overcome the world" (John 16:33, NIV).

Jesus is saying, yes, like Him, you will have some really tough times but take heart! Keep your eyes on the future that awaits believers, one of life, not death. He wants us to understand that while we're in the midst of these difficulties, we can look for the blessings that are in them and be comforted with the fact that they have a greater purpose. God always has an eternal perspective in regard to our trials and burdens. While they may be arduous, they aren't allowed into our lives to hurt or discourage us but to grow us. From God's perspective, they're a blessing. Our human perspective thinks it's a curse. But we need to tell ourselves that our lives are not at all about getting everything we want, when we want it, and how we want it. It is about fulfilling God's will for our lives, however He sees fit to do so, even—and especially—in the trials.

God loves to give us good things but these good things he gives us, more often than not, are of a spiritual nature, with immeasurable worth. In other words, that which will help the sanctification process—to cleanse us and make us more like Christ.

Jesus gave us everything by not quitting when things got indescribably painful, but continued through to the end, on the other side of the difficulty, to where the greatest blessing was: in the fulfillment of God's will for His life. He experienced a level of emotional anguish that is described in Luke 22:44, "And being in agony he prayed more earnestly; and his sweat became like great drops of blood falling down to the ground."

He submitted to unbearable physical agony as nails were driven through His hands and feet. Since it was customary to place a sign above all criminals to identify the charge for which they were being crucified, Pilate wrote "Jesus the Nazarene, King of the Jews." (Remember, the religious leaders accused Him of blasphemy.) Written in three languages, little did he know when he inscribed those words that it was 100%

true that Jesus is King—of all!

It's sobering to put this in perspective on a much more personal level. In reality, since I am one of the sinners that He died for, I should have been insulted, spat on, flogged, tortured, betrayed and denied. The cross should have been occupied by me. My hands and feet should have had nails driven through them. I should have gasped for air and suffocated. My side should have been pierced by the sword. And the inscription on the sign at the top of the cross should have read "Jennifer the Sinner, Enemy of God."

In identifying me, the words would be 100% true as well, in every sense and in every language. That's also the case for your name and the name of any human being ever to exist.

That is, if it weren't for Christ.

Praise be to God that's not the story!

Jesus isn't a quitter.

Because His name was on the cross, ours never have to be. Because there is salvation in His name, we bear a new name: "Child of God."

I think it's interesting and a noteworthy observation (but certainly no accident, in my humble opinion) that perseverance is first on the list of what suffering produces. It's not necessarily more important but perhaps a foundation from which to build the others. You will need perseverance to continue strengthening your character and building up hope.

Let me remind you of the definition for perseverance: "the continued effort to do or achieve something despite difficulties, failure, or opposition" and "the action or condition or an instance of persevering: steadfastness."

Steadfast is defined as "firmly fixed in place: immovable; firm in belief, determination, or adherence: loyal." [8]

The first definition is more general as it relates to navigating through our sufferings and the strength with which we do it. The second is specific to our faith: the holy thread that is woven into each circumstance of our lives. It's the sanctification process as well as holding on to that which God has promised is waiting on the other side, just like what Abraham and many others in the Bible did. It's what Christ did.

I pray it's what you will do, whatever your burden today, tomorrow or next year. Persevere. You'll need to hold tight to the Savior. It may be scary at first to not try to manipulate the outcome. It may seem ridiculous to hope against hope.

But believe me when I say, nothing could be further from the truth. The more you step out in trust, the more you find it's worth every second.

WORTH EVERY SECOND

:04

Gone Running

I'm a runner. I wasn't one until about twenty years ago, when I set a goal to run my first race after our third son was born. I was always active growing up and into my young adult years, whether it was cheerleading, softball, racquetball or biking. Even throughout my pregnancies, I worked at staying fit. But running's my thing; it's my jam. Truly, there is no "high" like a runner's high for me and it can't be replicated with any other activity I engage in. I'm not terribly fast but I have stamina and dogged determination. I'm the tortoise, not the hare, and quite frankly, the longer I run, the better I feel.

You may or may not know that a marathon is 26.2 miles. I've not run one—yet. It's on my bucket list, though. I've run half-marathons and I'll save you the trouble of being distracted with doing the math; it's 13.1 miles. I've also run plenty of 5-mile and 3.1-mile (5K) races.

I've participated in several run streaks, something *Runner's World* magazine challenges its readers to do over the holidays. It starts the day after Thanksgiving and continues through New Year's Day and the goal is to run at least one mile each day. It's a great way to remain committed to health and exercise during what should be called the stuffing season, not the holiday season. The vast majority of us seem to make a sport of stuffing ourselves without excuse. If it were an Olympic sport, I'm pretty sure that on several occasions I would've been standing on the winner's podium. I've never understood how I can spend the better part of the year treating my body like the "temple of the Holy Spirit" that it is (1 Corinthians 6:9) and then abruptly shift to the other end of the spiritual spectrum of becoming a "lazy glutton" (Titus 1:12) for five solid weeks. Apparently, there are plenty of others who step onto the merry-go-round of debauchery based on the *Runner's World* streak challenge. It's of little consolation to know that I have so much company.

But I digress. I almost forgot where I was going with this.

I tell you these things because each distance has its own set of challenges; in addition, each race course has its own as well. But they all carry the same goal: to cross the finish line, preferably upright and uninjured.

There are so many factors to consider when preparing for a race in order to ultimately make it across the finish line. There are things you can control (what you wear, what you eat, your training) but a very strong possibility exists that something will happen on race day that you cannot control and at that point you have two choices: give up (quit) or gut it out (persevere).

Which option you choose will depend on how bad you want to reach the finish line, how committed you are to reaching your goal and how willing you are to do the hard work in order to reap the reward. It's in every racer's best interest to not only train their body but also their mind. My mantra during my most recent half-marathon race was *how bad do you want it?* It was a cold, rainy October morning and I had to repeatedly ask myself that question. I've found my body will keep going as long as my mind doesn't give up. I don't know any athlete that hasn't had to make a decision in regard to pushing themselves past the proverbial wall from time to time.

And so it is in life. Every person has challenges, each day different from another. Many factors play into what we need to navigate through them and there are things we can—and cannot—control. And, without question, there will be circumstances that will push us to our limits. The question is still: do we give up or gut it out? How bad do you want it? For instance, how deep is your desire to have a better marriage? Enough to choose forgiveness, humility and repentance? What about lose the extra weight in order to be healthier? Enough to meal prep and schedule your exercise? How much do you aspire to get better grades in school? Enough to pay attention in class and effectively prepare for exams? How bad do you want to experience less anxiety and fear in your life and have it replaced with more peace and joy? Enough to open your Bible daily to meditate on what it says and commit it to memory?

In all cases, what steps are you willing to take to prohibit yourself from making excuses along the way?

All of these things take work and they require sustained focus on the One who will give you the strength to walk through the fires, wade through the deep waters and overcome that which oppresses you. (See Isaiah 43:2.) Don't try to avoid obstacles or squirm out of them. Don't just stand there paralyzed with fear and don't retreat. Go through each one with Him. Perseverance needs to be developed, practiced and perfected so if it seems like you keep going through something over and over or you haven't yet received what you've been praying for, just keep pushing through. The wall is only so thick. I am convinced of God's faithfulness and He will bless us abundantly when we allow Him to work these character traits into our lives. It is amazing; not easy; but amazing! More than anything I want to be able to say, "I have fought the good fight, I have finished the race, I have kept the faith" (2 Timothy 4:7, NIV).

To put on a race event, volunteers are needed. They are the ones doing everything behind the scenes and along the course route to help the participants get through the race. They not only offer a cup of water, Gatorade or package of Gu Energy Chews but words of affirmation, too. Every race I've ever been a part of has also had spectators along the road who cheer the runners on. There's nothing like seeing the handmade posters and hearing the shouts of "*You're doin' great! Almost there!*" Some people have noise makers, some are taking photos and little kids are jumping up and down, clapping their hands when they see their mom, dad or sibling coming around the bend. It's really quite a spectacle to be a part of.

You know what I think? I think Jesus is our biggest

cheerleader and I am convinced He'd want us to know that whatever we face, we can rest assured that He is there with us, and not just as a spectator. No, He's running the race right alongside us, shouting *You're doin' great! Almost there!* How could I ever quit with that kind of encouragement? I love Hebrews 12: 1-3, because it revitalizes me on so many levels:

"Therefore, since we are surrounded by such a great cloud of witnesses, let us throw off everything that hinders and the sin that so easily entangles. And let us run with perseverance the race marked out for us, fixing our eyes on Jesus, the pioneer and perfecter of faith. For the joy set before him he endured the cross, scorning its shame, and sat down at the right hand of the throne of God. Consider him who endured such opposition from sinners, so that you will not grow weary and lose heart" (NIV).

Why is all of this support important to us runners? Because it's grueling work, no matter the distance. Yes, we sign up for it. I've had many people tell me they wouldn't run unless a bear was chasing them. That's fair. I get it. Racing is emotionally and physically challenging. It's draining in every sense of the word and a test of our resolve. Always, we keep our eyes on the finish line. It's the prize we've spent months (for some, years) preparing for and with each step, we are making a conscious decision to endure in order to grab hold of it. The encouragement, noise, and excitement all feed us and help us to push through the fatigue and doubt.

I've learned that half the battle is actually making it to the starting line because sometimes our bodies just don't cooperate. We get hurt. We aren't feeling well. Nevertheless, if we do make it there, we fully intend to give it our best effort.

Unfortunately, there is the dreaded "DNF" in the running world: "Did Not Finish." Most have at least one or two in their careers. I've not yet but my brain and body both have tried to talk me into it on several occasions. Sometimes it's just one; other times, they team up on me. Anyway, for those who have had to stop, there's got to be no bigger disappointment. For whatever reason, they were unable to continue and I've seen the anguish on their faces. Yet, if they've been running for any length of time, they know it's just part of the sport. They'll determine to keep lacing up their shoes and fill out another registration form in the near future.

For those who reach the finish line, there's no feeling more satisfying. It's such a rush of emotions—relief, elation and an appreciation of seeing what our bodies are capable of accomplishing. When I cross the finish line, I am pumped up, smiling from ear to ear, sometimes crying, and always thankful to be alive, grateful I *get* to run. The announcement of my name as I cross, the time on the clock and the cheers of the crowd (whether for me or not) are the culmination of my desire to reach that which was one, five or ten miles up the road that I couldn't yet see but I knew was there. It was coming. I just needed to take one step after another after another to get there.

Fix your eyes on Jesus. Consider Him. Why? So that you won't grow weary and in turn, lose heart. Keep taking the next step in your faith and then the next and the next. Run your race well, with purpose and always keeping the prize in mind. He'll bring you to the finish line and if need be, carry you across it. And let me tell you, that finish line is going to beyond our wildest dreams. Keep an eternal focus, dear soul. Keep imagining what it will be like to hear the Lord say to you, "Well done, good and faithful servant. You have been faithful over a little; I will set you over much. Enter into the joy of your master" (Matthew 25:23). Though the race may be long and difficult, we will receive the reward of our faith. "And after you have suffered a little while, the God of all grace, who has called you to his eternal glory in Christ, will himself restore, confirm, strengthen, and establish you. To

48

him be the dominion forever and ever. Amen" (1 Peter 5:10-11).

And when we have the joy of stepping over into the presence of our Master, it will be worth every second.

Get Out of the Boat

I have a dear friend who faced something so devastating in her life that I can't even begin to fathom the pain she was forced to endure.

I won't go into all the details but right after this tragedy, brokenhearted and in pain, she often walked with her head bowed down in sorrow. When her teenage son would see her like that, he would lovingly reach out, lift her chin up, and say, "Mom, lift your head." It was his way of redirecting her attention upward. Every time he saw her head down like that, he would repeat those words and gently lift her chin to look into her eyes. This is an exponentially beautiful and loving thing for God to do: provide comfort and encouragement through her young son.

That image of my friend's caring and compassionate

son is how I imagine Jesus is with us. When we are experiencing the sufferings of this world, He reaches out, lifts our chins up and says gently, *Lift up your head. Look- at -me. And. Don't. Stop.* And like her son, Jesus will reach out time and again to remind us.

It reminds me of the story we read in Matthew 14:23-32:

"And after he had dismissed the crowds, he went up on the mountain by himself to pray. When evening came, he was there alone, [24] but the boat by this time was a long way from the land, beaten by the waves, for the wind was against them. [25] And in the fourth watch of the night he came to them, walking on the sea. [26] But when the disciples saw him walking on the sea, they were terrified, and said, "It is a ghost!" and they cried out in fear. [27] But immediately Jesus spoke to them, saying, "Take heart; it is I. Do not be afraid." [28] And Peter answered him, "Lord, if it is you, command me to come to you on the water." [29] He said, "Come." So, Peter got out of the boat and walked on the water and came to Jesus. [30] But when he saw the wind, he was afraid, and beginning to sink he cried out, "Lord, save me." [31] Jesus immediately reached out his hand and took hold of him, saying to him, "O you of little faith, why did you doubt?" [32] And when they got into the boat, the wind ceased. [33] And those in the boat worshiped him, saying, 'Truly you are the Son of God.'"

There is so much to learn in this portion of Scripture that I'm sure I could write a whole book just on these few verses. Maybe I will one day but today is not that day therefore, I'll briefly break them down so as not to miss what the story is telling us.

After having served thousands of people in multiple ways, Jesus retreats to pray to His Father (verse 23). This is our first important lesson: we should be sure we retreat to pray to the Father for direction and respite—always, but especially when feeling overwhelmed. Second, the disciples were in the midst of being battered by waves as they attempted to make it to the other side (verse 24). Third, Jesus will come for us (verse 25). Fourth, when we're terrified, He will reassure us of Who He is (verses 26, 27). Fifth, as silly as it may sound, when we need Him to prove it, He doesn't mind that we ask (verse 28). And when we do, He's incredibly gracious and indulgent. *Come*, He tells Peter (verse 29).

Let me expand on this for a bit. Peter got out of the boat, which if you really think about it, took great faith! He was so impulsive, sometimes wanting to unabashedly live *for* Jesus and other times out of wanting to prove himself worthy *to* Jesus. I'm not sure how I would've reacted in that moment—on one hand, if Jesus were right in front of me telling me to walk toward Him in the middle of a turbulent sea, I probably would have excitedly done it without thinking, too. I can be a lot like Peter. Why in the world did he doubt? Notice he was easily walking on water, experiencing the power of God firsthand. It wasn't until he took his eyes off of Jesus and looked at the storm swirling around him that he began to sink, right?

Do you see? It's all about His power, not ours.

What happens in Mark 4:37-39 displays this same power: "A furious squall came up, and the waves broke over the boat, so that it was nearly swamped. [38] Jesus was in the stern, sleeping on a cushion. The disciples woke him and said to him, "Teacher, don't you care if we drown?" [39] He got up, rebuked the wind and said to the waves, "Quiet! Be still!" Then the wind died down and it was completely calm" (NIV).

We're no different in that we, too, have been blessed to witness God's power in our lives which begs the question, why do we doubt? For the same reason Peter did: we look at the storms, with their wind, waves, and rain instead of on Jesus. In our fear, there's a tendency that we'll try to take the reins away from God, like Abraham did (see Chapter :03).

Because we aren't patient enough to wait on Him, we miss the opportunity to watch as He causes the wind to die down, the waves to stop crashing and the driving rain to subside. We are also unable to perceive the presence of His peace since we are too busy with the details of devising our own escape route. God's is too much like little Billy's, right?

I read this encouraging tidbit from Richard Blackaby on Twitter (@richardblackaby) in a reference to Mark 4:38: "In the storm, it is always comforting to notice Jesus serenely asleep in the back of the boat!"

That's really good, don't you think? Look to Jesus. What is He doing? He's praying, thanking, waiting, believing and yes, resting. No, not from protecting, guiding, or working but from worrying. Yes, what the disciples were going through was a real storm. There's no question about that but choosing not to worry doesn't equate to denying. It means you take the storm, add God to it and the sum is peace in it.

Is this your response when an issue blindsides you on some random Tuesday at 7:23 a.m.? Typically, the first reaction to difficulty is to complain, resist it and lament how the bed of roses we'd hoped for is instead (seemingly) a thicket of briars. But that thicket of briars is a treasure trove of opportunity for spiritual growth, if we'll choose to see it that way. No, it may not feel as good going through them as if we were walking on rose petals but remember that those same roses have thorns. What do you choose to see when you look at a rose bush? What do you choose to see and how do you choose react to that which is troubling you? With panic? Fear? Self-pity? By cursing out God?

I sincerely hope it's none of these things because I believe He's telling us, *Listen, if you'll just trust me and be patient, I promise I'm going to show you something amazing but you will have to walk with me through this first.* And in my mind, I picture Him lovingly taking our hand, leading us and saying, *Come, let me show you.*

I hope you'll pray as David did in Psalm 61:1-4: "Hear my cry, O God, listen to my prayer; [2] from the end of the earth I call to you when my heart is faint. Lead me to the rock that is higher than I, [3] for you have been my refuge, a strong tower against the enemy. Let me dwell in your tent forever! Let me take refuge under the shelter of your wings!"

When something that could cause a derailment of my faith arises, I've learned to immediately pray *Lord, You knew this was going to happen and you've allowed it for a reason. I trust you. Tell me how to glorify Your name in this.* It doesn't

56

eliminate the problem, but it puts me in a position of receiving what God wants to teach me.

Trust God to do what only He can do. Take your eyes off the storms around you, get out of your boat and walk toward Jesus in bold faith. But should you find yourself losing your focus, cry out to our Savior. He will immediately rescue you from worry and fear. I pray you'll take pause with each burden and ask the Lord to help you see things from His unlimited field of vision instead of your tunnel vision. I know it's worth every second.

WORTH EVERY SECOND

:06

Bread & Fish

I once read in *Runner's World* magazine, "Triumph cannot exist without strife." Think about that statement for a minute. If you don't have strife, then what, exactly, are you triumphant in overcoming? The fact of the matter is there is no desire for healing if there first isn't sickness. There is no understanding of joy if there isn't an opportunity to mourn. And we certainly won't recognize a miracle if there isn't a need for one in the first place. There must be a reference point for one in order that the other has meaning.

If we read about the account of Jesus feeding the five thousand, I believe we can see ourselves in the disciples:

[15] As evening approached, the disciples came to him and

said, "This is a remote place, and it's already getting late. Send the crowds away, so they can go to the villages and buy themselves some food." [16] Jesus replied, "They do not need to go away. You give them something to eat." [17] "We have here only five loaves of bread and two fish," they answered. [18] "Bring them here to me," he said. [19] And he directed the people to sit down on the grass. Taking the five loaves and the two fish and looking up to heaven, he gave thanks and broke the loaves. Then he gave them to the disciples, and the disciples gave them to the people. [20] They all ate and were satisfied, and the disciples picked up twelve basketfuls of broken pieces that were left over. [21] The number of those who ate was about five thousand men, besides women and children" (Mathew 14:15-21, NIV).

Meeting the demand of so many people with so little supply was a problem only to the disciples.

It wasn't for Jesus. It certainly was no surprise to Him. And He knew that the One who is the Source of all supply was able. Do you believe that in whatever you face? Let me remind you that we have the same God available to us. In our darkest moments, the Source is able to provide us with all that we need. Doesn't it seem logical that the reason Jesus said what He did in verse 16 was because He wanted them to see past what was available to them from an earthy standpoint in order to see what was available to them eternally? Do you not think He does the same to us? He knows both the trial we'll face and the solution He has already provided. When we question and fret, He will tell us matter-of-factly what to do. But will you act on what the Word says or on your own perception of the situation, which appears to be an insurmountable hurdle? Will you be like the disciples and protest? If you do, He'll simply say, "bring it to me" and then show you what He's capable of (verse 18-19).

A lengthy search for the original writer of *Just a Closer Walk With Thee* turned up conflicting accounts of who actually wrote it but Kenneth Morris (1917-1988) is credited with researching the song and having determined that it wasn't yet published, proceeded to arrange and release it in 1940. [9]

The chorus of the hymn requests,

"Just a closer walk with Thee,
Grant it Jesus, is my plea
Daily walkin' close to Thee
Let it be, dear Lord, let it be."

The words are vocalizing a desire for a deeper relationship with the Lord and all of the blessings that come with it and yet, when He tries to accomplish this type of intimacy through a trial what is typically our first reaction? Did we not ask for this when we sang the words? I understand that sometimes we sing songs out of habit, without really considering their meaning but surely we should know what we're saying whenever we worship God (singing is an act of worship).

It's like how there's the propensity to recite the Lord's Prayer with little emotional response because the words are familiar and repeated so often: "Pray then like this: 'Our Father in heaven, hallowed be your name. [10] Your kingdom come, your will be done, on earth as it is in heaven [11] Give us this day our daily bread, [12] and forgive us our debts, as we also have forgiven our debtors. [13] And lead us not into temptation, but deliver us from evil'" (Matthew 6:9-13). Our prayers can become diluted if we aren't careful. Also, our prayers carry weight and we might not even realize the gravity of them. Here's an example: When you pray this prayer, do you really mean, 'your will be done'? Do you realize that His will is whatever He deems to be suitable and good for our lives, not just that which is easy or pleasurable? Do you understand when you breathed those words that He's going to answer that prayer and probably not at all as you envisioned; not with what you want but what you need?

The disciples didn't necessarily need more bread and fish, they needed a deeper understanding of who Jesus was. They needed to be a part of a miracle in order to grow their trust and in wisdom. If you have a problem trusting the Creator of the universe, the Alpha and the Omega, Who was and is and is to come, then who is it that you think you *can* depend on? "Jesus said to them, 'I am the bread of life; whoever comes to me shall not hunger, and whoever believes in me shall never thirst'" (John 6:35).

The point I'm trying to make is to be keenly aware of what you're professing to the Lord God Almighty. Our mouths, hearts, minds and souls should be meshed with God's. Our worship, prayer and service should never become rote. Regularly ask God to reveal to you when any aspect of your walk has become routine. Ask Him to ignite a fire in you. Jeremiah 20:9 is a deeply meaningful verse to me: "But if I say, "I will not mention his word or speak anymore in his name," his word is in my heart like a fire, a fire shut up in my bones. I am weary of holding it in; indeed, I cannot" (NIV). We want to live bursting at the seams for Him. We want not just burning embers but a fully engulfed, twenty-alarm fire raging inside us. We want an outpouring of love, joy, peace, patience, kindness, goodness, faithfulness, gentleness, self-control (Galatians 5:22-23). He deserves nothing less.

Trusting in God is a win-win. He's never late, never too tired, never stumped. When you feel like you can't make it another day—or another minute—tap into His deep well of provision. There's nothing like it. It's what I would describe as soul-drenching: the capability to flood our very being with every life-giving good gift at just the right time in the exact measure we need it. It is poured into us and has the ability to move mountains and free us from our bondage of worry, fear and discouragement. Like races courses, while all have challenges, some will seem exceedingly rocky, uphill and miles long. This feeling will be notably magnified if we're try-ing to do it alone, which, by the way, the Lord never com-manded nor expects us to do. So, if you think you're doing a fabulous job all by yourself, I am going to sweetly and boldly tell you that attitude isn't Biblical because it's indicative of a spirit of pride. I can bear witness to the fact that choos-ing to do life without God isn't wise and there will be un-pleasant ramifications for that choice, namely frustration, dysfunctional relationships and anxiety. All in heaping doses.

(Read the first chapter again if you need to.)

I don't know what you're in the throes of today, but I do know God promises that He will faithfully be beside you. Maybe you're mourning the loss of a loved one or facing a health issue. Perhaps your son or daughter is a prodigal. Could it be that your spouse isn't a believer and you want salvation for their soul? Have you yourself never believed in Jesus as your Savior? Have you given up on God in the midst of your exhaustion and despair? You certainly wouldn't be alone if you were experiencing financial stress because now more than ever, in this day and age of COVID-19, people are losing jobs and incomes. The number of people with addictions, whether to drugs, shopping, pornography or bitterness, has increased substantially.

Whatever it is, do not for one single second listen to the devil's lies. God is for you and loves you. If you're being told anything else, don't you believe a word of it. Do not to give up, dear, sweet soul. Here's why: If we keep our eyes on Jesus, who perfects us, and if we desire to know God on a deeper level, remember that even if it's a more difficult road, it's still a better route to take than to travel an easy road all the days of our lives and never grow spiritually. How regrettable it would be to never allow sanctification, especially since that's what our Christian lives are about—to become more like Jesus each day. He assures us it will be worth every second.

:07

Love Notes

As I write this, I've been married to Brian for almost 30 years. Really, it's just a drop in the bucket when you consider my grandparents were married just shy of seventy-one years. My parents will celebrate sixty years of marriage in the next few months. That's such a blessing—and perseverance!

During the time of our courtship and marriage, we, like everyone, have had ups and downs, good times and bad. There have been words said that never should have been uttered, hurt inflicted on each other that can be forgiven but not completely forgotten and nights I cried myself to sleep, both because of what was done to me and also because of regret over what I'd done to him.

But we have persevered and quite honestly, I love him more today than when I first met him. Back then, I didn't think it was possible to love him any more than I did. But, as is usually the case, the more you seek to know someone, the greater the depth of connection.

I can tell you this, though: Marriage isn't for the faint of heart. It's no cake walk. Unfortunately, too many enter into it expecting the unreal perfection and happiness of a fairy tale, each one's idealized fantasy different, depending on whether it's concocted in the mind of the man or woman. *It's so cute when they leave their wet towel on the floor. I don't mind picking it up.* Until the 50th time and then it isn't, and they aren't cute at all but rude and sloppy. *Their snoring is adorable. It doesn't bother me.* Until, after three months straight of it, you're sleep deprived and your mind starts to envision solutions that may have jail time attached to them.

Funny, isn't it? The so-called "honeymoon stage" of blissful ignorance over your spouse's annoying habits rarely lasts long enough before one or the other becomes discontented. Without hesitation, we move into areas of unreasonable expectations that lead to disillusionment. I'm not trying to be negative; quite the contrary. I'm freely sharing honesty in this public service announcement. It shouldn't be a discouragement but a prompt to expect rough seas for which an anchor should be obtained and a life preserver grasped.

The encouragement comes now: when we're anchored in Jesus, there is nothing we can't get through.

The thing is, it's not wrong to hope for a great marriage. I don't know anyone personally who entered into it with the sole purpose of walking out of it. It's not wrong at all to see past the faults your spouse has, the problem comes when you won't. It's not foolish to expect happiness you've never experienced before, because you will. The problem occurs when your happiness is dependent on what they do instead of what Christ did. I'm sure you've heard it before but in case you haven't, happiness is based on your circumstances, which change frequently. Joy, on the other hand, is found in Christ alone and is never shaken. It's the condition of your soul that is characterized by an ability to be unmoved in the midst of life's earthquakes. One of my favorite Scriptures comes from Ephesians 6:14-17: "Stand firm then, with the belt of truth buckled around your waist, with the breastplate of righteousness in place, [15] and with your feet fitted with the readiness that comes from the gospel of peace. [16] In addition to all this, take up the shield of faith, with which you can extinguish all the flaming arrows of the evil one. [17] Take the helmet of salvation and the sword of the Spirit, which is the word of God. [18] And pray in the Spirit on all occasions with all kinds of prayers and requests" (NIV). We can't withstand the shaking without standing firm in our battle gear. I gave to my Bible study group the name "Stand Firm." It reminds us to put our armor on so we won't become unstable in our faith. It's also on my dining room wall and a social media hashtag I attach to my posts quite regularly. To me, it is one of the most important principles of our faith, one that needs to be nurtured and practiced consistently. Stand firm. Even just saying it out loud gives me a sense of strength and realigns my heart and mind.

I find it interesting: in a way, wanting a fairy tale marriage is precisely what you'll get since every story has conflict. What most people correlate to this type of writing is the ending, when you arrive on the last page and discover that good wins; that's why it's called a happy ending. It's what our mind focuses on as we close the book, forgetting that there was tension and strife that the hero or heroine had to triumph over. While we were reading those portions, we were rooting for the underdog, expectantly waiting for truth to reign and evil to be defeated.

Speaking (sort of) of dogs, I'm of the mindset that we should be more like dogs because they give us unconditional love, are always glad to see us, and are quick to forgive.

There's a joke I once heard that underscores this concept. It goes loosely like this: A dog will love you more than your wife. If you don't believe that, lock them both in the trunk of your car for thirty minutes. When you open the trunk, which one is happy to see you? I can't speak for every wife but I would say if my husband did that to me, I guess I'd say thanks for allowing me the company of my awesome pooch.

This isn't a deeply theological statement on which to build your faith but I think God created dogs so we could see how to treat others. My years of experience with canines has proven this to be true. I challenge you to find one and watch its behavior. Pay attention to its reaction after you angrily yell at them in the heat of a weak moment because they were just being themselves, doing dog things. They aren't angry in return. They don't bark back at you. They wag their tails, lick your face and forgive you. Further, they don't bring it up three days down the road by giving you the cold shoulder or sleeping in the other room.

Or consider when you've left them alone all day. When you walk through the door you don't get a lecture. You get your very own welcome home party. Not just once. Each time. The moment they see your face, their memory of your long absence is erased. They're just grateful to see you. Us people, well, we would do well to adopt that perspective with those that we care about because it seems we just can't help ourselves. We bemoan the terrible offense and can't muster the strength to just be grateful our family member is alive and walking through the door.

But I digress. Thank you for allowing me the latitude in sharing my very important opinion on dogs. I'll get back on track now.

We can't forget there will be conflict within all of our relationships. It is inescapable to have human interactions and not experience differences of opinion, disagreements and hurt feelings. This is precisely what human beings *do* forget, patently *want* to forget. Serve up an ooey, gooey heaping of happy and throw everything unpleasant into the trash. Can we all just agree that life does not work that way? I've come to understand that it doesn't and still believe it's beautiful because it has God's fingerprints all over it.

I want to share the birthday card Brian recently gave me because it sums up exactly what a marriage is.

"As I look back today on all that we've shared, there's nothing that I'd want to miss, Not one smile, not one frown, not one up, not one down, not one word, not one touch, not one kiss... For it took everything, all the goods and the bads and the just- in- betweens put together to make you and me what we always will be—the two most in love people ever."

Our relationship is stronger and I feel truly blessed to have gone through everything with him. I have learned so much. Within our relationship are the hard and ugly things but obviously there has been forgiveness, grace, love and the desire to work through the not-so-desirable things.   I pray every day for my husband, our marriage and for us to continue to work at it, through ALL of it, because do you know why marriages break up? Because one spouse—or maybe both—decide not to persevere. I mean that as no condemnation at all if anyone has experienced a break up. I speak from personal experience. My first marriage ended in divorce. For a while I felt immense shame. I was young, immature and unprepared for the relationship. I was also unwilling to forgive or offer grace for faults and failings. I gave up, that's what I did. So, here's what I'm saying:

The breakdown of a marriage begins in that moment someone refuses to do the hard work.

Let me stop here for a minute. I've known plenty of people who wanted to save their marriage but it didn't turn out that way. They wanted to do the hard work. They suggested marriage counseling. They offered to change if only given another chance. They prayed and pleaded with God to mend the broken bond, to reconstruct the trust. (Note: abuse of any kind should never be tolerated.)

But sadly (and all too often) the other person wasn't as invested. The other person is now legitimately the problem. Unfortunately, they hold the keys to the future, so to speak. Their choices are the beginning of the end. They refuse to do things God's way and decide not to work through that difficulty, that hurt, or that disappointment.

Ultimately, each one builds upon another until there is a sturdy wall between them that seems unable to be scaled and a wedge so deep it seems impossible to remove.

Technically, that's one hundred percent true. They can't be scaled or removed if both husband and wife aren't rooted in the God of miracles.

Let's be honest, it isn't "irreconcilable differences" that breaks couples up. There is no such thing when the God of the universe is allowed to get involved. God is The Great Reconciler. Just look at what He did for mankind through Jesus. If He can do something as magnificent as that, you'll never get me to believe He can't reconcile two people who have been joined together in His sight. The real reason is, that after those words are spoken, and the inevitable problems arise down the road, they then decide not to seek His perspective at the most critical crossroads. They choose not to ask for His help in restoring the beautiful sacred union they entered into with Him, rejecting the idea of asking God to heal it, as if it isn't even an option.

As if He isn't able.

Believing that lie leads to heartbreak, shattered families and emotional turmoil that plagues the souls of all involved for months and years to come. Through Jesus Christ we receive salvation and eternal life. So, since He "is able to save to the uttermost those who draw near" (Hebrews 7:25) how is it conceivable to believe the marriage is unable to be salvaged and given new life? How could it be true that when those involved draw near, they would not be given the tools to save themselves from their own destructive behavior and attitudes?

Referring to the Romans 4:18 through 5:4 portion of Scripture (see chapter :03), we only seem to want the justification, peace, grace and hope, the feel-good part in our faith, right? Not the suffering part. That's just like us: we want the joy of the resurrection but not the agony of the cross. For Jesus, there was no joy without first going through the agony.

WORTH EVERY SECOND

The person who declares that they want only the good times, for better, for richer and in health, all things rosy and perfect is forgetting to consider what Christ endured. Their response to an issue that seems as high as a mountain indicates that their focus is on it rather than on the Mountain Mover. They spurn the bad times, for worse, poorer or in sickness and shirk the responsibility of their vows when the scale isn't tipped their way. Oh, how quickly the memory fades when it comes to remembering the promise made to God that the covenant would be honored "until death do us part."

Regrettably, they missed out on the blessings waiting on the other side of each and every difficulty and in the fulfillment of God's will for their lives.

If only they would believe that the One Who raised Lazarus from the dead can also resurrect a marriage.

If only they would ask God to give them a renewed love in their heart for the person they gave their heart to.

If only they would stop, take a breath and ask God for clarity.

If only they would ask for the Holy Spirit to fill them to overflowing with gratitude.

If only they would ask for a desire to want the will of the

Father, as Jesus did in the Garden of Gethsemane before He willingly went to the cross. His love for us was the motivating factor to continue. The events of Christ's last days on earth, with betrayal, denial, beatings, a sham trial and ultimate crucifixion was anything but rosy. He wore a crown of thorns that represented the weight of our sins upon Him. Does any obstacle we face even come close? For crying out loud, can't we get past much more trivial things? Can't we, too, allow love to motivate us, as it did for Christ? Further, why not do it all because of our love for Christ?

The apostle Paul obviously did. Here's the short list on what he endured for Christ: "Five times I received at the hands of the Jews the forty lashes less one. [25] Three times I was beaten with rods. Once I was stoned. Three times I was shipwrecked; a night and a day I was adrift at sea; [26] on frequent journeys, in danger from rivers, danger from robbers, danger from my own people, danger from Gentiles, danger in the city, danger in the wilderness, danger at sea, danger from false brothers; [27] in toil and hardship, through many a sleepless night, in hunger and thirst, often without food, in cold and exposure. [28] And, apart from other things, there is the daily pressure on me of my anxiety for all the churches" (2 Corinthians 11: 24-28).

We most likely won't ever experience any of these things but if, like Paul, our focus is on the right Person, with our determination to keep the faith, the result is that everything else is taken care of, whether relationally, emotionally, spiritually or financially.

Shortly thereafter, Paul gives the account of how he was caught up to the third heaven. (This is where God dwells, in the unseen realm; the first is the atmosphere, where we'd see birds flying; the second is where the sun, moon and stars reside.)

What a high that must've been!

Years down the road, he was inflicted with a thorn, in order that God might work on Paul's humility.

"Three times I pleaded with the Lord about this, that it should leave me. [9] But he said to me, 'My grace is sufficient for you, for my power is made perfect in weakness.' Therefore I will boast all the more gladly of my weaknesses, so that the power of Christ may rest upon me. [10] For the sake of Christ, then, I am content with weaknesses, insults, hardships, persecutions, and calamities. For when I am weak, then I am strong" (2 Corinthians 12: 8-10).

Seems like this would be a low but you see, it's all about where his strength is coming from. Please don't miss what

Paul concentrates on. He asked to have it removed but was told "no" three times. He decides then and there that if God has decided the thorn will work out His plan better, he's okay with it. Actually, he says he's "content" with all that he's facing. This is a perfect example of "glory-ing" in our sufferings.

It often doesn't feel like we can, does it? We keep asking God to remove our own thorn(s), but to no avail. So be it. Continue on through the mud and muck. Feels like your shoes might come off? Let them. Just keep plodding. Feels more like quicksand? Keep reaching out for the Vine. He won't let you be sucked under. It's in relying on His ability that we learn to be content.

Dear, sweet soul, it's certainly not that we can't stand firm in our faith or navigate stressful relationships; we can, with God's help. It's just that we may become so weary in the fight that we give up. But never forget that God's grace is always sufficient because His favor is never insufficient.

I had said that I loved Brian more now than when we first met. That's because all of our highs, lows, and in-betweens have solidified our bond. Each one has taken us to deeper levels of unconditional love, understanding, compassion and mercy that never would've been possible had we not persevered. How *could* any of those things have a chance to

develop if we hadn't given each moment or season an opportunity to play out? How can we see God's restorative
power at work if we don't allow Him the time and space to
do so? Since God's timetable is different than ours, maybe
God was just rolling up His sleeves, so to speak, when we
decided to call it quits. Gee whiz, we didn't even afford Him
the time to get His healing hands in there to begin!

I can't imagine a closer earthly relationship than the one
I share with Brian. That's as it should be when we take those
vows. But I never could've been acquainted with this level of
closeness if I had quit. And because I believe in being honest,
there were times I wanted to. By the grace and power of
God, I didn't. And neither did Brian.

The same is true of my relationship with Jesus. When I
first met Him, I was so in awe, so interested in all He had to
say and I drank Him in. I spent my free moments with Him.
I talked with Him throughout the day. I couldn't wait until I
could sit alone with Him and *just be*. I soaked up His Word
like a sponge and wrung it out on anyone who would listen.

And now? Even more. *So much more.*

See, despite the trials I've faced, the Lord has taken me
to deeper levels of love for Him, a richer understanding of
His ways, renewed hope time and again as well as abounding

reverence, trust and obedience. Yes, I have learned the same things in my joyous moments but that's just it: life isn't one or the other. It's the sum of the whole. I'm so thankful for that. I'm also able to be confident that the challenges on the horizon will prove to take me deeper still. I know that the God I serve is faithful.

I can't imagine a closer, more important relationship than with Almighty God. That's as it should be. Above every human relationship comes the one with Whom all others are created. He gets top billing. "I am the Alpha and the Omega," says the Lord God, "who is and who was and who is to come, the Almighty" (Revelation 1:8). He deserves to be first. After all, union with Him was designed and ordained by Him so that we could experience a love like no other.

So far removed from any likeness to our earthly relationships, there are no hidden annoying habits to uncover with Jesus. There aren't any surprises coming down the pike about His character or behavior. "Jesus Christ is the same yesterday and today and forever" (Hebrews 13:8). We won't get three years into our relationship with Him and discover He isn't everything we'd hoped for. No, as it turns out, He encompasses every single thing we could ever want or need. The honeymoon stage never, ever ends. And I have never,

ever wanted to quit on Him.

Consider the zealous love He has for us, shown in infinite ways. I won't list them all here but lovingly guide you to the Scriptures. You'll find from beginning to end the love note God wrote to us is drenched in genuine, unrivaled affection for us, His creation. Each and every one. If you have a heart beating in your chest, His love for you knows no bounds. No matter the size of your home, the brand of clothing you wear, the bottom line in your checking account, how tall or short, buff or not so much nor what your checkered past (or future) looks like. He doesn't use any worldly things as the measuring stick of His love and even more important to remember is that neither does He determine His level of love based on our sins. We would all be in trouble if that were the case. But it's not.

Not even close.

Romans 8:35-39 is such a beautiful description of His agape love: " Who shall separate us from the love of Christ? Shall tribulation, or distress, or persecution, or famine, or nakedness, or danger, or sword? [36] As it is written, 'For your sake we are being killed all the day long; we are regarded as sheep to be slaughtered.' [37] No, in all these things we are more than conquerors through him who loved us. [38] For I am sure that neither death nor life, nor angels nor rulers, nor things present nor things to come, nor powers, [39] nor height nor depth, nor anything else in all creation, will be able to separate us from the love of God in Christ Jesus our Lord." Too bad the same can't be said for human relationships. You don't have to look far to see people allowing some small matter come between them, sometimes for years or for forever.

In 1 Corinthians 13, Paul gives his readers a model for what love should look like. These certainly aren't the only verses that tell us how to love one another like the Lord but he really hones in on the importance of love. Since God is love (1 John 4:8,16) doesn't it make sense that love would be paramount to anything else we could offer another human being? Go ahead and read it for yourself. Ask God to help you live it by the power of the Holy Spirit. "And it is my prayer that your love may abound more and more, with knowledge and all discernment, so that you may approve what is excellent, and so be pure and blameless for the day of Christ, filled with the fruit of righteousness that comes through Jesus Christ, to the glory and praise of God" (Philippians 1:9-11).

If someone were to read the love letter you have penned for those around you by how you live, what would it say?

Would it be filled with contempt and complaints? Unfor-giveness and selfishness? Perhaps envy, arrogance and bit-terness?

What a pity that would be. Christ didn't die on the cross for that.

I choose daily to persevere in my marriage and in every earthly relationship. Because my focus is on Jesus, the peo-ple I am in contact with become the recipients of Jesus' love and all that it embodies. They are the beneficiaries. Because God's grace is enough for me, I am able. Because I am able through Him, there's always a harvest for the Kingdom.

Especially, I choose to persevere in my union with Christ. You know what? Each time I choose His way and the more I opt to implement His principles, the more natural it becomes to love like Him. In case you're wondering, no, it isn't ever too late to begin to love as radically as Jesus does. The cost of choosing the opposite is far too steep. Choosing love and perseverance will never disappoint us. When they are inter-twined in how we relate to others, we'll find that any and all investments we make in people—and in Jesus—are worth every second.

:08

Out of the Blue

When I first starting writing this book, I had no idea I would be including this story in it. To be honest, I wish I wasn't.

Yet, the very fact that the book is on the Biblical principle of perseverance and the blessings that come from our trials, it seems incredibly fitting that the principle would be put to the test. It's not only been a learning experience for me in how to steer through the confusion and concern (both my own and my son's) but also in standing firm in my faith so as to be an encouragement. To be Christ's ambassador. To walk the walk in real time as I talk the talk or, technically, as I write the words. I praise God for the opportunity to see Him at work.

Our oldest son, John, recently and abruptly began to have difficulties with his eyesight. He described it as he had looked at a bright light and the remnants of the image remained. Frightening and concerning, to say the least.

He was sent to an ophthalmologist who found lesions in his eyes that were rapidly spreading. Each week he went back to have his eyes dilated and scanned in order to document any progression. Without question, had they reached the optic nerves, there would be complete, permanent vision loss.

In addition, he was encountering other symptoms that we didn't realize were connected and ultimately, John was also referred to a dermatologist and rheumatologist. Upon examination and further testing, he was diagnosed with psoriasis and psoriatic arthritis. It all made sense now. About a year ago, his palms were so split, it made work extremely difficult and painful. Mind you, he is part of the family's construction and remodeling business so he kind of needs to use them. When he sought medical advice, he was first given instructions to moisturize more and use gloves. When that didn't help, he was then given an ointment to lather on them. Still no improvement.

I'm grateful in this season of COVID that he was able to be seen by all of them rather quickly and ultimately begin treatment. I fully believe that was God's handiwork.

The correct treatment for his hands has given him relief and complete healing of the symptoms that those with the condition experience.

In addition, the medicine prescribed for his eyes has prevented the lesions from progressing. As it stands now, there is scarring in both eyes, in different places within each one, but he is still able to see, albeit with some difficulty. He most likely will need corrective lenses to bring his eyesight as close to 20/20 as possible. While he struggles to read clearly the words on a page, for the time being his eyes seem to be compensating for one another. He remarked recently that if this is how he has to live the rest of his life (with the level of at which his vision is now), he'd be fine with that. He's grateful he didn't lose all of it. To God be the glory always.

The debilitating joint pain associated with psoriatic arthritis has been the hardest thing for him to come to grips with. At the onset, he struggled to carry out even the most basic day to day activities let alone the rigors of construction. Many days he didn't.

The physical upheaval that occurred as each component took its toll on his young body brought with it emotional strain as well. His entire body was being affected and he wasn't getting any relief. If his body didn't remind him something was terribly wrong, his mind did.

From not only a human standpoint but a mother's, it was so heartbreaking to watch. Seeing someone suffer isn't anything anyone enjoys. When it's your child, it's compounded.

I can only imagine how Mary felt as she witnessed the horrific things Jesus endured.

I sent John a message that told him how sorry I was that he was going through all of this and that I wished I could do more to help. As a parent and a follower of Jesus, I boldly pray for complete healing (because, well, God could do that!) yet I also surrender my will to His. I believe and understand, as does John, that there is a divine plan being played out right now. It's something that God saw coming even if we didn't. He didn't stop it. That makes a lot of people angry. *If God is so good, then why didn't He stop it from happening?* they ask. My answer to that would be, yes God is good, oh so good. And then I'd add, it's because His plan is significantly better than ours.

This attitude of sheer confidence didn't happen overnight for me. It has been a process of being thrown into the fiery furnace and coming out perhaps with some soot but fully aware of God's precious, strengthening presence. Seeing Him through the flames. That's the stuff perseverance is made of.

"Therefore, since we are surrounded by such a great cloud of witnesses, let us throw off everything that hinders and the sin that so easily entangles. And let us run with perseverance the race marked out for us, [2] fixing our eyes on Jesus, the pioneer and perfecter of faith. For the joy set before him he endured the cross, scorning its shame, and sat down at the right hand of the throne of God. [3] Consider him who endured such opposition from sinners, so that you will not grow weary and lose heart" (Hebrews 12:1-3, NIV).

I certainly don't want anyone to ever grow weary or lose heart but to go directly, courageously and often to the throne of God to ask for help. That's the prescription for anything that ails us.

As I was out and about one day, I was praying for John. I had been thinking about how much admiration I had for him as he continued each and every day to get up and just *try*. Everything required effort. I know that his willingness to learn all he can about his condition and take appropriate action will pay off. He was still pushing himself to go for walks with his dogs. He was still going to worship the Lord. When he couldn't sleep in the middle of the night because of the pain, he was still turning to the Bible for comfort. He was still sending texts to me, asking for prayer. He wasn't quitting.

And that's when it occurred to me that this story should be included. I called and asked for his permission to do so. I shared my thoughts with him and offered this insight: he is an example of what perseverance looks like. He told me that he didn't think he was because he hadn't gotten through it yet. His response brought tears to my eyes.

In that moment, I was given the chance to provide him with encouragement because of what the Lord had taught me over the years. What he was doing is *exactly* what the Bible says perseverance is. It's steady persistence in our course of action *until* we get through the struggle, determining that no matter how long it takes we're going to keep trusting God *while in it*. Our victories come not just when we cross the goal line but with each successive yard towards it. Maybe it doesn't always look pretty but the progress forward is still sufficient enough to warrant a celebration.

Although my son is experiencing this, there is much to be grateful for: his loving and supportive wife, medication for his condition that has begun to relieve the pain in his joints, a cozy home, food in the fridge, their jobs, their sweet pups, dependable family and friends and so much more.

I had laid flat on my face when he first started experiencing the vision loss and asked God to give it to me. *He's young, Lord, with so much yet to see*, I said as I cried. I shared my concerns with God: *He needs to be able to work, Lord, in order to provide for his wife* (as if God wasn't already aware). Not knowing his future, I still imagined that he would have his babies to behold. *Please, Lord, I've seen enough in my lifetime, more than I could ever have dreamed I'd be blessed with. Let me have these issues. I can handle it.*

Turns out, so can John, by the power of the Spirit that lives in him. I knew that in my heart but naturally I want to shield those I love from harm. For that brief moment, I was forgetting what I knew to be true: living in a bubble, free from any field of thistles, is not really living at all. That would be atrophy—physical, mental and spiritual. I want God's will, for myself and all those I love. I know it's perfect. I know He has the answers we need. And I know I would be a fool to insist on removing any thistles from anyone's life, including my own, because He's just doing what He does best. Without exception, upon arriving through to the other side, comes sweet satisfaction, a sense of accomplishment and undeniable proof that even unexpected experiences are worth every second.

:09

Soar

Earlier I spoke about being a "reformed entitle-ist" (see page 22). We will never understand the concept of perseverance if we don't first get rid of the mindset that our lives are all about what we think we should have or deserve to have. It's neither desirable or appropriate to have that expectation of those around us or of God.

Let me boldly and sweetly say that we ought to be thanking our gracious Lord every second of the day that He isn't giving us what we truly deserve because that would be death—eternal separation from Him—because of our sinfulness. Can we all just stop right here, fling ourselves prostrate on the floor and praise Jesus because He didn't quit? That's where we get down to the nitty-gritty, where the realization of what we've been saved from causes us to live a surrendered existence for the One Who did the saving.

For those whose faith has been put in the Lord, God promises this in Isaiah 40:28-31: "Have you not known? Have you not heard? The Lord is the everlasting God, the Creator of the ends of the earth. He does not faint or grow weary; his understanding is unsearchable. [29] He gives power to the faint, and to him who has no might he increases strength. [30] Even youths shall faint and be weary, and young men shall fall exhausted; but they who wait for the LORD shall renew their strength; they shall mount up with wings like eagles; they shall run and not be weary; they shall walk and not faint."

While this portion of Isaiah is a message to the Jews in regard to their future exile (which means "separation"), it certainly is a timeless Truth for all believers. If God felt it was important then to prepare His people for their upcoming captivity and encourage them of His presence until they returned to their land, the same would hold true for His Church. God prepared His chosen people for the future and He does the same for us. Being separated from the Almighty because of captivity to sin, He sent Jesus to restore us to

94

Himself and until we meet Jesus face to face, He knew we would need to be reassured of His presence. That we would need strength. That we would know that the power of the Spirit is capable of taking us to new heights. That He could (and would) breathe new life into our circumstances.

Renew means to replenish. The footnote of my study Bible states it this way: "Find endless supplies of fresh strength." He fills us to overflowing again and again. Not just once or twice but each time we seek comfort. It's a promise to never leave our cup dry. That's not to say the cup won't be dry (only because we've allowed it be) but that each time we choose to ask for a refill, the cup overflows.

While out to eat, did you ever have a server who poured your glass of water a little too fast? Perhaps too much ice clogged the spout so the water behind it gushed out over it? All over the table? Maybe all over you? That's what our God does for us. *Endless supplies.* Do you believe that promise? If you don't, why not? Let me remind you that God never breaks His promises. Ever. The Word says when we wait on the Lord we will mount up with wings and soar like an eagle, we won't grow weary and He will replenish us. What, then is stopping us from holding on to this knowledge and persevering?

I have a few thoughts on that. Actually, I have a lot of thoughts, as evidenced by the many words of this book. I don't mean to imply that the ones I'm sharing are the only ones, but are, in my humble opinion, the most evident.

I hate to put Satan at the top of any list but I believe when we doubt, fret and crumble it's often because of his lies. The evil one would love nothing more than for us to be weak so that he can keep us down. He loves to do that because when he can get us to doubt that God will and get us to believe God won't, he has control over us. When he can get us to be all stirred up inside over what *may* be, he can keep us from peace. When he erects hurdles and throws obstacles in our path, he can keep us from taking the next step in our faith because of fear.

Another possibility is our own self-defeating, negative mindset. *Woe is me* we cry. We throw pity parties for ourself. No one comes except, well, Pity. Sorrow might tag along. Insecurity is a third wheel but doesn't care. They revel in the chance to be miserable together. And so, we say those two words that God the Father, Jesus the Son and the Holy Spirit never say: "We can't." If our hope is in ourselves, of course that's true. We should, instead, be affirming what Psalm 33:20-22 says: "We wait in hope for the Lord; he is our help and our shield. [21] In him our hearts rejoice, for we trust in his holy name. [22] May your unfailing love be with us, Lord, even as we put our hope in you" (NIV).

Another reason? Brace yourself because this may really hit home: we don't persevere because we're just being lazy. Proverbs 13:4 tells us, "The soul of the sluggard craves and gets nothing, while the soul of the diligent is richly supplied." Some synonyms for lazy include apathetic, halfhearted and listless. Go deeper and you find words like indifferent, spiritless, lukewarm, uninterested and even haughty. This is why I love to study words; looking at just one we might be inclined to believe we aren't *that*. Or even, in this case, we aren't *that lazy*.

But when we choose not to live according to His standards, we're not living up to our potential; especially, we fall short of God's intentions for us. This is particularly true for the aspirations He has for our journey of faith. Are you indifferent to or living halfhearted for Him? Do you lack excitement and boldness in drawing closer to Him? Are you so proud that you don't think you need to study the Bible? If we aren't studying the Word so that we can become spiritually mature and prepared we are, by definition, lazy. The key point here is that not knowing what the Scriptures say will affect every aspect of our life. We cannot depend on any-thing else, which is why Proverbs 3:5-6 urges us, "Trust in the LORD with all your heart, and do not lean on your own understanding. ⁶ In all your ways acknowledge him, and he will make straight your paths." Trust the Lord above all else. Lean on Him. He won't let you off the good paths.

So, how do we prevent these things from occurring in our lives? And how on earth do we do this perseverance thing? I hope that you've gleaned lots of good ideas already but to sum it up, read the Word, know the Word, practice believing the promises in the Word. And be diligent in doing so because then your soul will be *richly supplied.*

I'll give you a few specific, practical ways to accomplish this, but always seek advice from the Word of God in any given situation. It is the blueprint for our lives.

First, since everyone uses mantras these days, use the Scriptures as your mantras. Take a verse such as Jeremiah 32:27, "I am the Lord, the God of all mankind. Is anything too hard for me?" and declare it! Say something like this: *Yes! You are the Lord, God of all mankind. No, nothing is too hard for you and I thank you that you will help me through what-ever I face today!* I challenge you say that out loud right now and tell me you don't feel the power of the Holy Spirit rush

98

into your chest. Do you see how confessing this instead of a string of pessimistic thoughts can quickly put an end to the party that Pity, Sorrow and Insecurity threw for you?

Matthew 4, verses 1-11, tell the story of Jesus being tempted in the desert by the devil:

"Then Jesus was led up by the Spirit into the wilderness to be tempted by the devil. [2] And after fasting forty days and forty nights, he was hungry. [3] And the tempter came and said to him, "If you are the Son of God, command these stones to become loaves of bread." [4] But he answered, "It is written, "'Man shall not live by bread alone, but by every word that comes from the mouth of God.'" [5] Then the devil took him to the holy city and set him on the pinnacle of the temple [6] and said to him, "If you are the Son of God, throw yourself down, for it is written, "'He will command his angels concerning you,' and "'On their hands they will bear you up, lest you strike your foot against a stone.'" [7] Jesus said to him, "Again it is written, 'You shall not put the Lord your God to the test.'" [8] Again, the devil took him to a very high mountain and showed him all the kingdoms of the world and their glory. [9] And he said to him, "All these I will give you, if you will fall down and worship me." [10] Then Jesus said to him, "Be gone, Satan! For it is written, "'You shall worship the Lord your God and him only shall you serve.'" [11] Then the devil left him, and behold, angels came and were ministering to him."

I have always found such courage in these verses because of Jesus' example. What did He say each time the devil opened his lying mouth and spewed his twisted version of Scripture? By the way, this is exactly what he does to us, too. The message of the story is that Jesus was tired, hungry and feeling every human emotion as God incarnate. How easy it would've been for Jesus to punch that vile being into the Lake of Fire right then and there. But he patiently endured. He rebutted each lie with Truth. Three times He was tempted; three times he said "It is written." I have no doubt that had the devil tempted Jesus a million times, a million times Jesus would've used the words of the Father to put Satan in his place. That's diligence. It's perseverance. No matter how many times he tries to distract or confuse or deflate us, we should take the sword of the Spirit, which is the word of God (Ephesians 6:17) and beat him at his own game. It's possible, you know. How? We have been given the ability through Christ Himself: "Behold, I have given you authority to tread on serpents and scorpions, and over all the power of the enemy, and nothing shall hurt you" (Luke 10:19). Do you see how the evil one has no power to overcome us mentally, physically or spiritually unless we allow him to? We have the power of Christ Himself within us, so use it!

Second, 1 Thessalonians 5:17 is only three words but they're imperative for our defense: "pray without ceasing." Prayer brings about a peace and calm as we set aside our Martha to-do lists in order to take time to be like Mary and *just be* with the Lord. Just be still, just be open to hearing, just be willing to see what He wants to show us. Someone once remarked (in what I believe was out of frustration in their particular predicament), "I know, 'just pray it away'" as if prayer was my cookie-cutter response to any problem.

Well, it is my default response to every problem but it's anything but cookie-cutter. My prayers are deeply personal and unique to each supplication and event.

It's also anything but a trite suggestion to someone when they seek my advice. It's an action done out of trust, love and absolute certainty that each time I have a conversation with I AM, He hears. I AM is my closest confidante. I always go to Him first. In good and bad times (which are all subjective), I open the door to the Throne Room and seek advice and comfort. The point is, I pray. And my heart longs for you to pray, also. Pray in all things, without ceasing. Pray before. Pray during. Pray after.

Self-examination should always be a part of our growth so I have a few things I'd like to ask you in regard to your prayer life, if you don't mind. Oh, who am I kidding? I'm going to ask even if you do mind because they're important to consider. Here we go.

When you pray, do you find yourself praying for things to be the easiest route or the simplest solution? Have you even once asked God to allow a trial to linger a bit longer so that you can see what else He might teach you? Probably not and I understand. That's a difficult concept to think about, let alone say but nevertheless it's a radical way to pray that could open up new doors in your heart and in your life lived for God. No one was more radical in His living for the Father than Jesus.

Do you neglect to take time to dig deeper, perhaps pause a bit longer on what the last verse you read really said? We aren't supposed to spend our time in communion with a check list in one hand and a stop watch in the other. It's great that you read your devotion this morning but what did you learn?

Are you giving God an opportunity to speak or are you doing all the talking? If we will permit Him, He will share insights and wisdom that stretch our capacity to understand

His character that in turn develop trust.

I'll ask again: when you pray the Lord's prayer, do you really mean "thy will be done"? Remember, His will is whatever plan He deems to be suitable and good for our lives, not just that which is simple and pleasurable. Is it possible that you have an issue with trusting what His plan is, the very one you prayed to be done "on earth as it is in Heaven"?

Don't miss that the context of 1 Thessalonians 5:17 is "rejoice always" (v. 16) and "give thanks in all circumstances; for this is the will of God in Christ Jesus for you" (v. 17). These commands aren't unattainable. Quite the opposite, but only with the help of the Holy Spirit because our flesh can't comprehend on its own how it could be possible. Nor is it advisable. But as we submit to a prayer life determined to seek a deeper understanding of God, our natural, human tendencies slowly but surely are blown away like chaff. We become able to step on the narrow path with more and more confidence and more consistently.

In the midst of our daily lives, rather than run around scared and like a chicken with its head cut off, we decide that instead, we're going to fall to our knees and work it out with Him. Then we rise, more assured, steadfast and expectant that things will work out. Maybe it takes a day or week or ten years for God to work out His plan but remember that even if it seems slow, we're told to wait for it will come and not be delayed (See Habakkuk 2).

It's worth noting that even if we don't see the answer here on earth, the promise is that if we'll trust His timetable, which is never late, the reward of perseverance is life in Christ, abundant in the here and now as well as forever. "Let perseverance finish its work so that you may be mature and complete, not lacking anything" (James 1:4, NIV). The beauty of allowing perseverance to do its work and be developed is that either way, our souls are at rest.

In addition, Romans 8:26-28 confirms that we have help along the way as we wait: "Likewise the Spirit helps us in our weakness. For we do not know what to pray for as we ought, but the Spirit himself intercedes for us with groanings too deep for words. [27] And he who searches hearts knows what is the mind of the Spirit, because the Spirit intercedes for the saints according to the will of God. [28] And we know that for those who love God all things work together for good, for those who are called according to his purpose."

A third element to apply is seeking support from those around you who will persistently point you back to Scripture and help you to focus on Jesus. These are the people who will keep you from adopting the wrong perspectives. In your frustration, impatience and anxiety you may be tempted to want to hear what you want to hear instead of what you need to hear. Surround yourself with people who will listen with a compassionate ear without compromising the Truth. Be wary of someone who frequently steers you toward a victim mentality or whose advice is more their heartfelt opinion than Biblical doctrine.

Finally, and perhaps the most challenging approach, is to take the time to glory in your sufferings. There is no better way to draw close to God than to lift praise in the midst of a trial. Trust me on this. It will bless you because it takes your eyes off the trouble(s). Remember, fix your eyes on Jesus, like Peter on the water. There are plenty of Bible verses and songs that lift praises to God and just as many blessings surrounding us each day so I can't imagine we could ever run out of instances to bless His name even when we feel at our lowest.

A prayer I came across many years ago that still is a cry of my heart and soul is, *Lord, redeem my pain and work through it until it bears fruit that will never pass away.*

I don't know what each of you is struggling with this day, but whatever your pain, if you'll allow, God will take it and work through it so that you will bear fruit that is invaluable, both for your life, those around you and, most importantly, for the Kingdom of God. That's where everything should turn to—the Kingdom. The discipline of making this part of my prayer default has proven to have an enormous impact on my faith. It will on yours, too.

In most instances, you no doubt have a desired outcome of how your scenario will play out. I'd be willing to bet that you're believing for the best. Keep doing that—just be sure that the hope you have is in God's ability because that's where it needs to be.

Whatever it is, do not give up. Be bold and be specific in your prayers. Trust that God will give you wings. Continue to pray, rejoice, stay connected to other strong believers and give glory because no matter how it plays out, you can't go wrong when you make it all about Him. You will never regret keeping a Kingdom mentality. Open wide your heart, mind and soul so that He can continue to develop fruit. And keep watching for what God is doing while you wait because He'll show you that the waiting is worth every second.

:10

It's Not Over 'til It's Over

I know I haven't shared particularly devastating or gut-wrenching personal stories thus far. My examples have been relatively shallow and perhaps you have come to assume, *Well, it's easy for her to persevere because after all, she hasn't experienced very hard things.*

Not that this is a competition, because let's face it, there is enough heartache to go around and nobody wins in a competition like that but I'd like to sweetly tell you that you'd be assuming wrong.

My experiences with perseverance have been shaped throughout my life, allowing me to be convinced of just how incredible our God is. This perspective gives me hope for the future and strength in the present. But let me say that as I type these very words, my father is in the hospital. He has cancer and numerous health issues involving his heart and lungs. Couple that with the fact that he has the COVID-19 virus and it presents a potentially bleak outcome. My mom has it, too, although she isn't being hospitalized. Both of my parents are in their eighties and their decline over the last couple of years has been difficult to watch. Both have always been hard workers and yes, they've lived long lives but that doesn't mean my heart doesn't hurt. I trust wholly in God's sovereignty, in His perfect plan and I know that until each person takes their last breath on this earth, they have a purpose. I am also fully aware that we all must leave this earth one day. But still, it doesn't prevent the inevitable pain we feel when someone we love struggles against their uncooperative, aging selves or when we must say goodbye.

From the age of seven, my younger sister spent years in and out of the hospital due to her three bouts with leukemia. At the age of sixteen, she received an experimental bone marrow transplant that saved her life. Not everyone shares that same outcome; in fact, she saw many on her hospital floor battling in the same way who succumbed to the disease. Pretty sobering to watch as a teenager. Myself a teenager and freshman in college, I distinctly remember the night my roommates drove me from Clarion to Children's Hospital in Pittsburgh, way over the speed limit, because that night the prognosis was dire. Walking into her hospital room and seeing her laying there, so still, so serene, I thought she had passed away. It was horrible. Praise be to God she survived.

I remember there was a lot of support and love from our community over the years and seeing how and what my parents sacrificed—despite no guarantee of success—was powerful to watch as a young girl. It's even more so as an adult with children of my own. My husband and I would do exactly what they did if it would save any one of our son's lives. Hands down, no holds barred, without question. That's what love is.

My mother-in-law and our nephew passed away several years ago, both within a five-month span. Our nephew died suddenly at the age of seventeen in a car accident; my mother-in-law only seven months after being diagnosed with breast cancer. My father-in-law has Alzheimer's and seeing the slow progression into forgetfulness, knowing that it will only get worse, is something far too many families know.

I was molested in my early teens, harrowing not just for me at that stage of my emotional development but for anyone to experience and work through.

There was alcoholism in varying degrees on both sides of my family. I don't think I need to explain how detrimental any kind of addiction is to a family.

I struggled with low self-esteem, deep insecurities and bulimia.

There were the tragic suicides of my twenty-six-year-old cousin and one of my brother's closest friends, who was sixteen. The traumas affected me, of course, but seeing what it did to those left behind who were desperately trying to understand, was far more psychologically painful.

This list isn't exhaustive but a representation of the harsh realities this fallen world delivers to us all.

Subconsciously, all of these things left indelible marks on my mind and in my heart to the point that I tried to erase them using unhealthy and destructive means, something, of course, I didn't realize I was doing in the midst of them.

So, no—no one wins in the battle for who had (or has) it worse in this life. We all take our turn. We may or may not have the exact same issues as the next person but make no mistake, it is inevitable that we'll experience being in a quandary. If we aren't right this moment, we will be. If we've just come out of a complex situation, there will be another down the road. That's not negative, that's Biblical. Remember what John 16:33 says? "In this world you will have trouble. But take heart! I have overcome the world" (NIV).

I admonish you to have mercy on and patience with others. We're all just trying to get through life, to keep on keeping on and to do it without caving under the pressure.

Here's the point: over all my years, God was there. Maybe I didn't feel Him; but He was there. Explain how else I could've done it. The only explanation is mercy and grace shown with a depth that human minds can't comprehend, served up with an unconditional love and divine strength. I didn't—and couldn't—do any of that on my own. Period. He has never let me down and He'll never let you down.

If my claim of this isn't enough for you, that's okay. I have proof. The Lord has never let humanity down since the beginning of time because, see, His plan of salvation and redemption began long before you or I were even a thought to our parents. We were to our Heavenly Father, of course, and then, knowing what He knew, of how we'd live for anything but Him while wanting us to live for nothing but Him, still sent Jesus to die for each and every one of us. We'd do anything we could to save the life of our child(ren) but God sacrificed His Son to save all of us. Hands down, no holds barred, without question. That's what His love looks like. Now tell me: if He did that for you and me, why would He desert us in the tough times? Logically speaking, it doesn't make any sense whatsoever that He would. James 1:2-3 tells us, "Consider it pure joy, my brothers, when you encounter trials of many kinds, because you know that the testing of your faith develops perseverance." How on earth do we find joy in the trials of life? It takes some work but as we look to the One Who is above all and in all, we can trust the Lord to walk with us as we take each step, giving us the strength to persevere. I hope you'll believe that trials are actually blessings to us. Too many people have the idea that if God is so good, why does He allow not so great things to happen? That's precisely why—because He *is* so good. The whole package deal given to us is the same package deal that was given to Jesus. Romans 6:5 says, "For if we have been united with him in a death like his, we shall certainly be united with him in a resurrection like his." True, we don't need to pay the penalty for our sins because He did that for us but why should we have a life free from uphill battles?

If we're going to be followers of Jesus, how could we

possibly justify the belief that we should have a life of rainbows, unicorns, and sunshine while His life was one of persecution, hatred, thorns, betrayal and crucifixion for which there was no legitimate reason because He was innocent, both of any crime and any sin. It was a blatantly unjustifiable and undeserved punishment, driven by jealously, power and fear. Tell me, how can we reconcile those facts? We can't.

What we can do, however, is to embrace that suffering is a part of this life instead of clinging to the false teachings of those who claim that if you're a Christian, God will give you only good things and if you're suffering it's because you aren't one. In that context, it is absolutely false.

To be clear, everything God gives us, whether a valley or a mountaintop, is inherently good because that's all He *can* give. God is incapable of being unjust. Everything is for our benefit.

Paul clearly understood this when he said, "But whatever gain I had, I counted as loss for the sake of Christ. [8] Indeed, I count everything as loss because of the surpassing worth of knowing Christ Jesus my Lord. For his sake I have suffered the loss of all things and count them as rubbish, in order that I may gain Christ [9] and be found in him, not having a righteousness of my own that comes from the law, but that which comes through faith in Christ, the righteousness from God that depends on faith—[10] that I may know him and the power of his resurrection, and may share his sufferings, becoming like him in his death, [11] that by any means possible I may attain the resurrection from the dead" (Philippians 3:7-11).

After years of walking with my Lord, I understand it, too.

Let me encourage you with this: whatever you're facing, it's not over. I'd be willing to bet you wish it were. You've no doubt wished from time to time that life could be filled with ease and void of obstacles. That sounds pretty appealing, doesn't it? But then you'd be missing what perseverance accomplishes. In actuality, it's a really great thing that it's not over; that means God is still working out His plan in your life and in the lives of those around you.

It wasn't over right after Jesus was born. Any typical toddler or teen issues he faced didn't signal the end. Even as He uttered the words "It is finished" on the cross (John 19:30) it wasn't an indicator of finality. Oh, it was for sin and death but for God's entire plan, there was still so much more to the story! How sad and hopeless if the moment Jesus breathed His last breath on earth it would've been the last page of the book. But no! He rose three days later and even in that God says there's still more. He ascended to Heaven and then on the day of Pentecost sent His Holy Spirit to live in all believers. No one knows, except for the Father, when the Church (we who are Christians and still alive) will be caught up with the Lord so we won't have to endure the Tribulation. God's plan for His chosen people, the Israelites, to be regathered in be- lief is certain and even still, that's not the end of the story. Jesus Christ is coming back to reign as King!

Paradoxically, the true, beautiful and exciting end of the story is that there is *no* end since we shall live for eternity in the presence of the Almighty. God's story for the Son of Man is never, ever over; it's everlasting. So is yours and mine. Sandwiched between our physical birth and death is both joy and suffering. Remember, the good news is that Jesus died for our sins but was also resurrected. The good and the bad, intricately joined together. When we are in Him, we partake in both. The difference between those of us who have sur- rendered to the Lord and those who haven't is that the suf- fering will one day end for us, forever.

"Then I saw a new heaven and a new earth, for the first heaven and the first earth had passed away, and the sea was no more. ² And I saw the holy city, new Jerusalem, coming down out of heaven from God, prepared as a bride adorned for her husband. [3] And I heard a loud voice from the throne saying, "Behold, the dwelling place of God is with man. He will dwell with them, and they will be his people, and God himself will be with them as their God. [4] He will wipe away every tear from their eyes, and death shall be no more, neither shall there be mourning, nor crying, nor pain anymore, for the former things have passed away" (Revelation 21:1-4).

Don't be discouraged and don't quit! There is inconceivable joy that lies ahead. Paul considered any and all earthly gain should be counted as a loss and that knowing Christ Jesus as Lord surpasses each and every thing on this earth. It isn't about what you have; it's about Who you have. That makes all the difference how we navigate this life. Every dismal, exhausting experience from my past and each one to come in the future is bearable because my story—the one God wrote specifically for me—isn't over. This love story between my Creator and I will continue through eternity.

And so will yours.

With each step we take in our faith to shift our perspective toward the Author of our lives, we will come to find that each trial is irrefutably worth every second.

:11

Are You Ready?

I sure do ask a lot of questions, don't I? Well, I've always believed and have taught my children to ask questions. It's how we learn. It's also good to ask ourselves questions. As far as I'm concerned, I think it's completely normal to answer ourselves, too. That's just another of my humble opinions so take it for what it's worth.

Funny story—I can remember one morning I was talking to God, working some things out. As I mumbled things under my breath, I was startled to hear my son ask, "Who are you talking to?" I had no idea he was around the corner, just a few feet from me; not surprisingly, what he heard wasn't making any sense. Apparently, he couldn't piece together any of what I was verbalizing into some coherent thought that actually applied to him but he erred on the side of caution and asked anyway. I appreciate that but honestly, after eighteen years with me, I really don't expect him to assume that I'm talking to anyone else. It's pretty impressive—I am remarkably capable of carrying on in-depth conversations with myself. Years of practice have honed my skills. I tend to get thrown off when someone answers me other than me.

This was one of those times, though, where I was in the middle of a dialogue with my favorite Person to engage in dialogue with. I don't know for sure but I think he was relieved when he found out I was praying and he didn't need to stop what he was doing to listen to me. If I were a betting girl, I'd bet that many people over the years have been relieved when they didn't have to listen to me.

The title of this chapter is a question in regard to your faith. I include in all of my lessons an invitation to enter into a personal relationship with Jesus as Savior and Lord. It's the perfect ending to my books and any women's event I'm teaching at. It's also the perfect beginning to an abundantly beautiful and fulfilling life for anyone who chooses to accept and act on the invitation.

Are You Ready?

I talked a good bit about running races in an earlier chapter (see Chapter :04). Whether you know it or not, you're running, too. We are all traveling on this journey to eternity and it is a marathon of sorts considering what we must face in this life. Some will reach the finish line quicker than others but make no mistake, we will all spend eternity somewhere, it is only a matter of where.

I must be clear: there are only two options available: in the presence of the Lord or in the Lake of Fire.

Do you know which location you'll be residing in?

Did you know that you have complete control over your destination? By choosing to believe on Jesus to save you, an incredible and perfect future awaits.

Conversely, if you choose to reject the only One who loved you enough to die for you, then your future is dreadfully grim.

Don't believe anyone who says that there is any other way. There isn't.

Don't believe anyone who claims that you can live any way you want because a good God wouldn't send anyone to Hell.

You cannot live any way you want without consequences. Not only does God have parameters and expectations but fundamental societal criteria also exist so that every choice we make in life has a consequence, good or bad.

We should never abuse God's grace. Romans 6:1-2 says, "Well then, shall we keep on sinning so that God can keep on showing us more and more kindness and forgiveness? ²Of course not!" (TLB)

As far as God sending you to Hell, He actually doesn't. You choose to go there for eternity by choosing to ignore the gift of salvation found only in Jesus Christ.

It seems incredibly preposterous to me that someone would decide they'd rather live forever in a place that is incomprehensibly miserable, according to the Bible's details. But that is exactly what happens when a person chooses to mock God instead of revering Him. It is what the Bible warns of repeatedly: there is an established consequence for not believing Jesus is the Savior of the world.

That, in fact, is what determines where we arrive when we leave this earth. Whatever our choice, we seal our own fate.

We decide which camp we're in: we're either in the camp of believers or we aren't. We're either followers of Jesus or we're followers of Satan. Based on Biblical Truth, there is an outcome attached to each camp.

God has prepared the way to life eternal. If you choose not to accept it, your destination is clear based on God's Holy, Inerrant Word. No one is "sent" anywhere by God. He simply has graciously and lovingly given all human beings a free will to do as they please. Make no mistake, whoever finds themselves in Hell, is there by their own doing; they foolishly boarded the bus bound for endless torment and unimaginable agony. That makes me so sad.

To this point, I have spent almost half of my life telling others about Jesus Christ and praying for people to enter into a personal relationship with Him. I have prayed for people I know, for complete strangers and those still in their mother's womb. I have people that have been on my prayer list for decades in regard to their salvation. Even though it may seem like nothing is happening, I keep believing that God is working in their lives. In some instances, I've been blessed to see the evidence. In the case of strangers, I will most likely never know the effects of my prayers.

Nevertheless, I pray. Hard. I have also prayed that all eyes reading this right now would turn to Him before it's too late.

With love, I urge you: don't wait to make your decision.

None of us know the timing of our last breath on this earth. Once taken, there are no more chances and no opportunity for a do-over.

None of what I've told you should be perceived as a scare tactic. It's not how God operates and it certainly isn't how I do, either. I've lived long enough to know that trying to trick, frighten, shame or guilt someone into a relationship with Jesus is not the least bit effective. It usually has the opposite result.

It's my job to tell you the Truth and do it in love. I take the responsibility seriously and the privilege to heart. Souls are at stake and eternal futures hang in the balance. The fire in my bones and the desire to speak in His name continues to grow each day. I pray yours does, too.

With that being said, I want to invite you surrender your life to the Savior of the world, right here, right now, thereby allowing the Holy Spirit to fill you with strength (and much more) so that you may persevere. So that you can glorify God. So that you can have eternal life.

If you'd like to enter into a relationship with Jesus, please read on about how to do that. It's not difficult but it is life-changing and life-giving.

Are You Ready?

The following excerpt is from my website. As you read, I pray for God be more real to you than ever before and for the Spirit to stir in you a desire to know Jesus.

~ ~ ~ ~

Dear, sweet soul,

May I get personal with you? What do you believe—about God, Jesus, the Holy Spirit?

Maybe you're not really sure and, honestly, I can't do much more than teach you what I know, encourage you to take the next step in your faith and pray for you. But let me tell you this: You are a sinner. So am I. So is every other human being. I'm not trying to be mean; I'm just telling you what the Bible says in Romans 3:23: "For everyone has sinned; we all fall short of God's glorious standard."

Gospel means "good news"; Jesus IS the Gospel! He is indeed great news for us sinners!

"For God so loved the world that he gave his one and only Son, that whoever believes in him shall not perish but have eternal life. For God did not send his Son into the world to condemn the world, but to save the world through him. Whoever believes in him is not condemned, but whoever does not believe stands condemned already because they have not believed in the name of God's one and only Son" (John 3:16-18).

By believing that God sent His Son to earth (Christmas), that Jesus died on the cross to pay the price for our sins (Good Friday) and was resurrected to life on the third day, defeating sin and death (Easter), we have accepted the Gospel message of Jesus Christ and thus have expressed faith in Him. Only through Him do we have salvation (are saved from paying the penalty of our sins) and by the repentance of our sins (admitting them and turning from them) are we promised eternal life in the presence of our Lord.

The Christian faith is about having a personal relationship with Jesus, and because we do, we are filled with the Holy Spirit, Who helps us to live out the beautiful, unique and fulfilling plan God has lovingly laid out for each one of us.

I hope that as you consider what you just read, you'll believe the Truth and tell Jesus you BELIEVE.

When you choose to do so is up to you but if you haven't done so already, my hope and prayer is that you will right now. I promise, it's worth every second.

"Salvation is found in no one else, for there is no other name under heaven given to mankind by which we must be saved "(Acts 4:12).

Are You Ready?

If you aren't sure what to say or how to approach God, know this: He is waiting anxiously to hear from you! Simply pray from your heart, knowing that He hears you when you humbly seek Him. Below is a prayer; not a "magic prayer" or the only way to talk with God, but a GUIDE for anyone wanting some help to begin the conversation.

Remember, He's been waiting for you all of your life to get to this point and welcomes you with open arms.

Lord, I confess I have sinned and need Your forgiveness. Help me to turn from my sins and begin living for You. Jesus, I believe You came to earth, fully God and fully human, to be my Savior and Lord and I accept Your free gift of salvation, as displayed upon the Cross and in the Resurrection. Please help me to follow You from this day forward and be all that You created me to be. Amen.

If you have just prayed this prayer from your heart, "Therefore, if anyone is in Christ, the new creation has come: The old has gone, the new is here! "(2 Corinthians 5:17). Because of your willingness to repent of your sins and rest on the sacrifice of Jesus, you are born again and assured of eternal life in Heaven. How exciting!! While this is a wonderful and important first step, I encourage you to continue to grow as a disciple of Jesus Christ by studying the Bible, applying it to your life and allowing it to transform you. Also, connect with other believers who will help you on your journey, through Bible studies, fellowship and mission work. May God strengthen you and your faith!

In His love,
by His love
and only because of His love
I lovingly serve you,

Jennifer

Notes

1. "tribulation." *Merriam-Webster.com*. 2020. https://www.merriam-webster.com/dictionary/tribulation (April 2020).

2. "perseverance." *Merriam-Webster.com*. 2020. https://www.merriam-webster.com/dictionary/perseverance (April 2020).

3. *Unshakeable Hope*, Max Lucado (pg., 112; 2018, Thomas Nelson)

4. "glory." *Merriam-Webster.com*. 2020. https://www.merriam-webster.com/diction-ary/glory (April 2020).

5. Ibid.

6. "consecrate." *Merriam-Webster.com*. 2020. https://www.merriam-webster.com/dictionary/consecrate (May 2020).

7. "sanctification." *Merriam-Webster.com*. 2020. https://www.merriam-webster.com/dictionary/ sanctification (May 2020).
8. "steadfast". *Merriam-Webster.com*. 2020 https://www.merriam-webster.com/dictionary/ steadfastness (May 2020).
9. https://thescottspot.wordpress.com/2016/09/03/ just- a-closer-walk-with-thee

A Few Things

As with everything I'm called to do, it is always immensely gratifying to fulfill God's purpose for my life.

Jennifer Cadamore Ministries was a vision of God's since before He created me. He then prepared me by giving me the gifts and talents to achieve His calling of teaching girls and women about His Son, Jesus. He accomplishes His Will through me in a variety of ways, with all teaching opportunities inspired by the Spirit and in His time.

Each sweet soul that I am able to interact with at an event or online affords me the chance of encouraging them to know God personally through the study and application of His Word. I am fully convinced that the Bible is instrumental in transforming our lives and is utterly necessary for growth. Because of this confidence, coupled with a desire for others to observe it in their own lives, a Bible distribution outreach goes hand in hand with this teaching ministry. For more information visit jennifercadamore.com.

You'll also find multiple resources that will help you take the next step in your faith, including podcasts, devotions and a link to my *Butterfly Moments* videos on YouTube.

My devotional book entitled, *You Are Beautiful! Devotions to Help You Understand Your Worth & Purpose* was born out of my many years of insecurity and trying to find confidence in all the wrong things (and people). God showed me that simply because He created me, not only do I have sacred value, but that I am beautiful in His sight. The same is true of you and for every soul ever created.

I hope you'll grab a copy for yourself and for every girl and woman you know! (Available in paperback and eBook on Amazon.)

If you'd like to support the ministry with a gift, you may do so on the website by going to the "Gifts" page. Or, if you prefer, you can do so by mailing it to:

Jennifer Cadamore Ministries
P.O. Box 57
Sarver, PA 16055

A Few Things

Please know that any gift, no matter its size, blesses this ministry richly and allows it to continue. Thank you for your generosity! We seek God's face in using them to His glory.

Thank you for reading *Worth Every Second, Developing Perseverance in Our Faith.* I pray it has strengthened your resolve to stand firm and deepened your trust in the Lord!

Follow me on these social media sites:
Twitter (@jencadamore)
Instagram (@jennifercadamoreministries)
Amazon (Author's page)
YouTube (Don't forget to subscribe! It's free!)
I am also part of the Christian Women Speakers network (www.womenspeakers.com)

Especially, please join the ministry team in praying that God's Will is accomplished according to His purposes.

Not to us, O Lord, not to us,
but to your name give glory,
for the sake of your steadfast love
and your faithfulness!
(Psalm 115:1)

WORTH EVERY SECOND

You are loved.
Persevere dear, sweet soul.
Persevere!

WORTH EVERY SECOND

I waited patiently for the Lord; he inclined to me and heard my cry. He drew me up from the pit of destruction, out of the miry bog, and set my feet upon a rock, making my steps secure. He put a new song in my mouth, a song of praise to our God. Many will see and fear, and put their trust in the Lord.

Psalm 40:1-3

Journaling Pages

_____

_____

_____

_____

_____

_____

_____

_____

_____

_____

_____

_____

_____

_____

_____

_____

_____

WORTH EVERY SECOND

Journaling Pages

_____

_____

_____

_____

_____

_____

_____

_____

_____

_____

_____

_____

_____

_____

_____

_____

_____

_____

_____

_____

_____

_____

_____

Journaling Pages

WORTH EVERY SECOND

You don't need to be anything more
than who God created you to be.

Just Be.

jennifercadamore.com